INSIGHT GUIDES

Great Breaks

SNOWDONIA
& NORTH WALES

Contents

Walks and Tours

Travel Tips

North Wales' Top 10

From its rugged mountains, dark forests and glorious coastlines, to its medieval castles, slate caverns and vintage railways, here are the top attractions of this beautiful corner of Wales

▲ **Blaenau Ffestiniog** and Slate Caverns *(p.46)*. Atmospheric Victorian village high in the mountains, where visitors can go deep underground to explore the slate caverns.

▲ **Snowdon** *(p.56)*. This iconic mountain is the highest peak in both England and Wales, and a magnet for climbers and hill walkers.

▲ **Centre for Alternative Technology** *(p.94)*. This fascinating centre may date back to the 1970s, but it now seems extremely modern, with its focus on green ways of living.

▶ **Portmeirion** *(p.71)*. Fantasy Italianate village created by Clough Williams-Ellis and which featured in the original cult TV series, *The Prisoner*.

◀ **Bodelwyddan Castle** *(p.17)*. Historic house in Denbighshire that's set in pristine parkland and acts as an outpost of London's National Portrait Gallery.

▲ **Caernarfon** *(p.51)*. While best known for its magnificent castle, Caernarfon is also a busy holiday town with plenty of attractions and places to eat and drink.

◀ **Llandudno** *(p.18)*. This Victorian seaside resort is one of the jewels of North Wales, with a fine promenade, pretty gardens and some good shops.

▼ **Ffestiniog Railway** *(p.45)*. This 19th-century narrow-gauge railway started life carrying slate through the Welsh mountains, but now gives tourists a wonderfully scenic journey.

▲ **Harlech** *(p.72)*. Harlech's castle dominates the hillside town and overlooks a gloriously unspoilt swathe of sandy beach that is ideal for families.

▶ **Conwy** *(p.20)*. Charming little town with a mighty castle and well-preserved medieval walls, Conwy makes a lovely base for exploring.

Overview

Wild Places of Wales

The craggy mountains and green valleys of North Wales combine to produce some of the most dramatic, and wildest, landscapes in Britain. At their heart is Snowdonia

When the traveller and essayist George Borrow toured North Wales in 1854, he wrote: 'Perhaps in all the world there is no region more picturesquely beautiful.' A bold claim, yet one not hard to justify – and

one that is surely shared by thousands of visitors today. Elsewhere there may be loftier mountains, deeper lakes, greater forests and swifter rivers but rarely are they found in such unique combinations.

Today, while Welsh Black cattle and the ubiquitous Welsh Mountain sheep share their hillsides with walkers and cyclists, climbers and hang-gliders, farming continues much as it has for generations. The common place name *hafod* (or *hafotty*) meaning 'summer dwelling' recalls the old tradition of transhumance when stock was moved to higher pastures during the warmer months. Dry-stone walls snaking over ridge and summit date from the 18th and 19th centuries, separating valley from *ffridd* (mountain

pasture), one farm from the next.

North Wales may not boast the sunniest weather in Britain, but it might well boast some of the cleanest air, the most pristine countryside, the strongest sense of history – oh, and some of its loveliest beaches. It is undoubtedly a green haven for lovers of the outdoors, especially the northwest corner known as Snowdonia. Eryri's peaks are a thrilling presence: inspirational to explore by road, challenging to those who walk and climb. The great crags and gullies have become associated with Britain's best-known rock climbers and mountaineers. The northeast corner is less dramatic, but contains some gloriously unspoilt villages, pretty market towns and sublime, pastoral scenery.

LOCATION AND TOPOGRAPHY

Igneous rock along with volcanic ash, lava and shale from the Ordovician Period makes up much of the savagely beautiful geology around

Above: the path to Tryfan and its twin peaks, Adam and Eve.
Below: hiking up Snowdon.

Snowdon and Cadair Idris. Older Cambrian rocks are most evident in the mountains of the Harlech Dome bordering Tremadog Bay. But by far the most striking influence on the entire Snowdonia landscape has been that of glacial ice.

The Ice Age which began some 2 million years ago and ended around 10,000 years ago has left an extraordinary and highly visible legacy in Snowdonia. At times throughout that period of very cold climate cycles, great ice sheets thousands of feet thick spread from Scandinavia to Britain. Meanwhile, permanent accumulations of snow on higher ground spawned glaciers which slowly flowed downhill, grinding away the bedrock, smoothing out U-shaped valleys and depositing huge mounds of excavated material called moraines. Steeply hollowed basins known in Wales as *cwms*, usually now filled by lakes and surrounded by cliffs, were left behind in higher locations. In geological terms 10,000 years is merely the blink of an eye. The result is a mountain landscape little changed since the last glacier melted.

CLIMATE

Hills and mountains create their own weather. Okay – it's wet. In common with most of upland Britain, there is greater rainfall (snow in winter) here than over the adjacent lowlands. More than 185in (4,700mm) of precipitation have been recorded on the Snowdonia mountains in one year and even in a drought year 100in (2,540mm) is not uncommon. Temperature falls as altitude is gained – about 5°F (3°C) for every 1,000ft (300m). Snow often lingers on north-facing slopes above 2,000ft (600m) well into May. Winds are notoriously fickle, sometimes funnelling viciously through valleys and over passes, at

Above: view of Llyn Llydaw from the summit of Snowdon.

other times disappearing altogether in sheltered locations.

Snowdonia's climate – essentially a collection of mini-climates – is changeable throughout the year, with the best of the weather usually, though not always, to be found on the fringes of the hills. Higher villages and roads may be shrouded in mist for days on end while those in the lee of high ground bask in sunshine. In westerly or south-westerly weather, districts such as the Vale of Conwy and the North Coast are often fine while the West Coast and most of the mountains sulk under cloud and rain. Similarly, east winds produce favourable conditions over Anglesey and the Lleyn.

May, June and September are the driest months in an average year.

ECONOMY

Earning a living from the land in the rugged heart of Snowdonia has never been easy. Only the hardy Welsh Mountain sheep and Welsh Black cattle are able to withstand the harsh climate and convert rough grazing into profit for the farmer. Lambing extends from March well into April, after which each ewe and lamb will be driven up the hillside to range

ⓕ Welsh Slate

Much of Snowdonia's earlier prosperity rested upon slate: that impervious, blue-grey stone that splits so conveniently into flat sheets. The industry faded in the late 19th century and long-abandoned slate quarries still scar many a mountainside, particularly around Blaenau Ffestiniog, Bethesda and Llanberis. However, their narrow-gauge railways and workings have long become visitor attractions in their own right. High-quality slates are still produced in limited quantities and are much prized by designers.

Above: Llechwedd Slate Caverns at Blaenau Ffestiniog.

over its acre or so of ground. Shearing takes place during June and July.

While traditional agriculture continues in the more fertile valleys and lowland fringes, forestry and electricity generation (hydro, nuclear and wind power) contribute their share of regional income. Manufacturing industries too, including high-tech and independent television production companies, play an important role in the economy.

Below: wind turbine blade at the Centre for Alternative Technology.

ENVIRONMENT

The windy, high ground of North Wales makes it an obvious choice for the siting of onshore wind farms – particularly as much of the area is sparsely populated, and land is relatively cheap. The Welsh Assembly, keen to create a low carbon economy and 'green' jobs, wants to more than double the energy it currently generates from onshore wind farms. Visitors will certainly be aware of their presence, the nature of which divides opinion in both Wales and the UK as a whole: some see them as clean, green and harmless, others as noisy eyesores that can have a negative effect on birdlife.

Guide to Coloured Boxes

ⓔ Eating	This guide is dotted
ⓕ Fact	with coloured boxes providing
ⓖ Green	additional practical and cultural infor-
ⓚ Kids	mation to make the most of your visit.
ⓢ Shopping	Here is a guide to
ⓥ View	the coding system.

Food and Drink

You can eat practically anything you want in North Wales, especially in large settlements such as Caernarfon, which offers everything from Thai cuisine to traditional teas. You certainly won't go hungry, as portions tend to be generous. In recent years there has been a move to put local produce on menus, and this is worth seeking out – especially as it is often high quality and organic.

You have a wide choice of places to dine in North Wales – from hotels and restaurants with rooms, to neighbourhood restaurants, cafés and bistros. And don't forget the pubs, many of which serve good food and are particularly popular for Sunday lunch.

WELSH DISHES

North Wales is justly proud of its succulent mountain-bred lamb and black beef, as well as salt-marsh lamb that is reared around Harlech. However, many visitors also savour the region's seafood. The Conwy Estuary and Menai Strait, both shallow and strongly tidal, provide ideal conditions for the

Ⓢ Farmers' Markets

Going to a farmers' market is a great way to meet local people, as well as to pick up fresh local produce. They are held all over North Wales, some weekly (like that held each Thursday in Colwyn Bay), others monthly such as Anglesey's (Menai Bridge) and Dolgellau's (Eldon Square), the third both 3rd Saturday of each month, and Mold's (St Mary's Church Hall) on the first Saturday each month. For a list of Welsh farmers' markets, check out www.fmiw.co.uk.

Above: Wrexham farmers' market takes place once a month.

cultivation of mussels, delicious served in a white wine and cream sauce, while the rocky shores around Anglesey and the Lleyn Peninsula yield excellent oysters, crabs and lobsters. For colder days try *cawl*, a traditional meat, root vegetable and leek soup; or perhaps *lobscows*, a warming lamb broth.

Fresh local vegetables, including the iconic Welsh leek, are widely available, and there are some delicious Welsh cheeses to try. The latter are produced in the south and west of the country, rather than the mountainous

Above: Caws Mynydd Du cheese is handmade from sheep's milk.

north, but are well worth seeking out – particularly some of the soft goat's cheeses. The best-known Welsh cheese is crumbly Caerphilly. Cheese features in a number of Welsh dishes, such as Glamorgan sausages (made from vegetables, herbs and cheese), and Welsh rarebit, a tasty mix of cheese, mustard and ale that is then grilled on toast.

SNOWDONIA SPECIALITIES

Above: scone sundae from Cadwalader's Café in Llanystumdwy.

Different parts of Snowdonia have their own products: high-quality rosé meat from the Lleyn, and Cadwalader's celebrated ice cream (which originated at Criccieth in the 1920s but is now widely available) being just two examples. Then there is Halen Mon salt, a sea salt from Anglesey that is highly praised by top chefs. Morning coffee and afternoon tea provide opportunities to enjoy griddle-cooked Welsh cakes *(cacen radell)* which are flat, circular, fruited and spread with butter or caster sugar. Another teatime favourite is *bara brith*, a fruited tea bread.

The great Liberal politician and statesman David Lloyd George, who lived near Criccieth, relished simple Welsh country fare. Traditional recipes compiled by the Criccieth Women's Institute and first published after World War I included Steamed Snowdon Pudding under 'Recipes for the Favourite Dishes of the Prime Minister' section.

WELSH BEER AND WINE

Beer is still the traditional alcoholic drink in Wales, the main brewery, Brains, is based in Cardiff in the south. To sample a real North Wales beer, look out for Purple Moose beers, which are brewed from an independent brewery in Porthmadog. The

landscape of the north is unsuited to vine growing; however, there are vineyards in South Wales where viticulture dates back to Roman times. Cariad Wines, from Llanerch, and Tintern, Parva Wines, from Tintern are the producers of some increasingly acclaimed whites. Also look out for Welsh mead, a fermented 'honey wine' made with honey and water: it's sweet – and often unexpectedly potent. A surprising addition to the Welsh drinks market came in the year 2000 when Penderyn distillery opened near the Brecon Beacons in South Wales. It produces a single malt whisky, as well as a Brecon gin and a Brecon vodka. It's certainly worth seeking out in specialist stores.

Find our recommended restaurants at the end of each Tour. Below is a Price Guide to help you make your choice.

Eating Out Price Guide

Two-course meal for one person, including a glass of wine.

£££	over £25
££	£15–25
£	under £15

Tour 1

The North Coast and Carneddau Mountains

This tour, which takes you from the pastoral Vale of Clywd to the heart of Snowdonia, is around 87½ miles (140.5km) long and is ideally done over two days

Lying beneath the Clwydian Hills is the lush Vale of Clywd, a pretty corner of Wales that tends to attract few tourists – despite being dotted with charming villages and historic churches. This tour starts here, in the market town of Ruthin, then sweeps down to the lively resorts of the north coast, where the A55 speeds you on to Llandudno, one of Britain's finest Victorian seaside resorts.

Further on you drive through the beautiful Vale of Conwy, a gentle landscape of fields and woodland leading to the darker conifers of Gwydir Forest and tumbling rivers around Betws-y-coed.

Later, your route takes you by the

Highlights

- Ruthin
- St Asaph Cathedral
- Llandudno
- Conwy
- Betws-y-coed
- Capel Curig
- Llyn Ogwen

Carneddau mountains, described by Thomas Pennant, in his famous *Tour in Wales* published in 1778, as 'very disagreeable, of dreary bottoms or moory hills...' Tastes change and many hillgoers now choose these sprawling

Preceding Pages: walkers on Mount Snowdon. **Left**: Conwy valley. **Right**: Nantclwyd y Dre, Ruthin.

whalebacks to escape the crowds on Snowdon and other popular peaks. Few roads penetrate far into these remote northernmost hills of Snowdonia, yet on every side they are bounded by scenery of extraordinary contrasts.

THE VALE OF CLYWD

Ruthin ❶, pronounced 'Rithin', is a charming market town in Denbighshire that sits at a strategic point on the River Clywd, and is brimming with Welsh history. Edward I built a castle here in the 13th century, which was later besieged by Owain Glyndwr (who burned most of the town as well), as part of his bid for an inde-

pendent Wales. In the Civil War, the castle became a Royalist fortress, but was eventually surrendered to Parliamentary forces – that soon destroyed most of it. The ruins were eventually incorporated into a 19th-century castle, which is now an hotel.

The castle is reached via Castle Street, which is home to **Nantclwyd y Dre** (tel: 01824 709822; Apr–Sept, Fri, Sat, Sun and Bank Holidays, 10am–5pm), the oldest timbered town house in Wales, which dates back to 1435. Furnished 'period' rooms are devoted to different ages of the town's history: there are Georgian and Jacobean bedrooms – the former with fine Chinese wallpaper – a Victorian schoolroom, and a hallway from 1942.

Notable amongst the town's historic buildings is **Ruthin Gaol** (Clwyd Street; tel: 01824 708281; www.ruthingaol.co.uk; Apr–end Oct Wed–Mon 10am–5pm). Constructed in the 17th century, it was in use until 1916, and has now been reborn as a visitor attraction. In Victorian times, a wing was built in the same style as Pentonville prison in London. You can see the cells, learn about the lives of the prisoners, what they ate and how they were punished. One 'star' prisoner was John Jones, known as the Welsh Houdini. He made a rope from his

bedding to escape from Ruthin Gaol – but is said to have died of shock after being shot whilst on the run.

LLANRHAEDR

From Ruthin, pick up the A525, and drive north to the hamlet of **Llanrhaedr 2** in the Vale of Clwyd, which sits just on the left of the road. The church here, **St Dyfnog's**, is famed for its stained-glass Jesse Window, which was completed in 1544 and is considered to be the finest in Wales. The window depicts Christ's family tree, showing his ancestors as far back as Jesse, the father of King David. It was removed during the Civil War to save it from rampaging Parliamentarians.

St Dyfnog came here in the 6th century, and if you follow a path from the churchyard to the woods, you can still see the Holy Well in which he would stand all day as a penance. It was once known for its healing properties.

DENBIGH

Continue on the A525, branching left onto the A543 to reach **Denbigh 3**, a market town whose name translates as 'little fortress' in Welsh. The town was a medieval centre of Welsh power and a residence for the Welsh princes. When Dafydd ap Gruffudd led a revolt against the English Crown, Edward I unleashed his forces, and in 1282 took the town, captured Dafydd (who was later executed), and charged his commander Henry de Lacy to build a castle on the remains of the prince's stronghold. **Denbigh Castle** (www.cadw.wales.gov.uk; Apr–Oct daily 10am–5pm, Nov–Mar until 4pm; charge when staffed), which sits on a hilltop above the town, is one of the largest in Wales; its most striking feature is a triple-towered gatehouse. The town walls were built at the same time as the castle. The castle fell into disrepair, and in the 16th century Eliza-

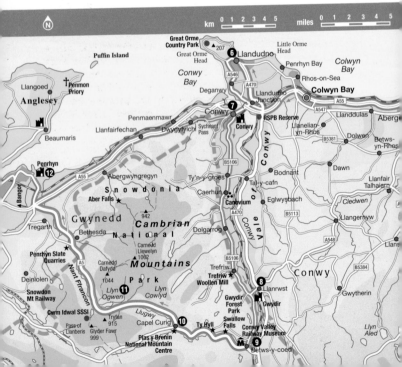

Above: Bodelwyddan Castle, a regional outpost of the National Portrait Gallery.

beth 1's favourite, Robert Dudley, was granted a lease on it. However, after the Civil War the castle deteriorated further and is now largely ruined.

Just outside Denbigh, on the A543, is **Gwaenynog Hall** (tel: 01745 812066; June–end Aug, by appointment; voluntary donation), the garden of which was the inspiration for Beatrix Potter's *The Tale of the Flopsy Bun-*

nies. With apple and pear trees, and large herbaceous borders, the garden is still much as it was when Beatrix Potter painted it.

ST ASAPH

Returning to the A525 and continuing north, you soon reach **St Asaph** ❹, which might look like a small town, but is actually a city thanks to its **cathedral** (High Street; tel: 01745 582245; daily). Dating back to the 13th century, this is the smallest cathedral in Britain, and sits on a site that has been a place of worship since AD 560. Inside is a superb collection of Welsh Bibles, including one by William Morgan, who was the first person to translate the Bible into Welsh. Only 800 of these were ever produced. Morgan is said to be buried somewhere in the churchyard.

BODELWYDDAN CASTLE

From St Asaph continue to join the busy A55 going west, to reach **Bodelwyddan Castle** ❺ (tel: 01745 584060; www.bodelwyddan-castle. co.uk; Sat–Sun Nov–Feb 10.30am– 4pm, Mar–Oct until 5pm, end Apr– end Oct Tue–Thu 10.30am–5pm, school holidays 10.30am–5pm, until 4pm spring half term). Built in the 19th century, on the site of a much earlier structure, Bodelwyddan Castle is more

Above: St Margaret's Church, also known as the Marble Church.

stately home than castle and once belonged to the Williams family who made a fortune in lead mining. During World War I it became a recuperation camp, while part of the grounds was turned into an area for trench warfare training (you can still see the trenches in the parkland today). After a period as a girls' school, Bodelwyddan was opened to the public in the 1980s, and is now a regional outpost of the National Portrait Gallery, displaying works by artists such as William Holman Hunt, George Frederic Watts and Ford Madox Brown. Furniture from the Victoria and Albert Museum is also on display.

Opposite the castle, on the other side of the A55, is the **Marble Church** with its soaring spire. Built in the 19th century, it gets its name from the 13 different types of marble used in the interior. The churchyard contains the graves of World War I Canadian soldiers who had been billeted nearby. The majority died from the Spanish flu pandemic, but

five were shot during the Kinmel Riot of 1919. Troops waiting to be sent home had rebelled when their ship was diverted to Russia.

Continue driving west along the A55 and you soon reach Colwyn Bay, one of the waterfront resorts that dots this stretch of coastline. Its Victorian pier still stands, though now exhibits rather faded grandeur.

LLANDUDNO

From Colwyn Bay rejoin the A55, continue west, then turn right on the A470 to reach **Llandudno ❻**, which lives up to its reputation as one of Britain's finest Victorian seaside resorts. Today grand hotels fronted by a broad promenade sweep round North Shore to the splendid Pier without an entertainments arcade or fast-food outlet in sight.

The town's early success prompted entrepreneurs to construct Marine Drive, a toll road encircling the Great Orme limestone headland which overlooks the town. It incorporates a **Bronze Age Copper Mine** (tel: 01492 870447; www.greatorme mines.info; mid-Mar–end Oct daily 10am–4.30pm). The mines were first discovered in 1987, and archaeologists gradually revealed a maze of tunnels dating back 4,000 years. The highlight of the self-guided tour is the cavern, which was dug out using stone and bone tools. In 1902 a **Tramway** (tel: 01492 577877; www.great ormetramway.co.uk; Apr–Sept daily 10am–6pm, Mar and Oct until 5pm) was laid to the Great Orme's 680ft (207m) summit, complemented more recently by a Cabin Lift (Easter–Oct daily, weather permitting), the longest in Britain. To savour this magnificent headland, walk round the perimeter wall from the car park, a distance of about 2 miles (3km); there are wide views over the Conwy Estuary to dis-

Above: view of Llandudno's seafront from its pier.

tant Anglesey, the Carneddau mountains and even the Isle of Man. The **Great Orme** is a country park and Site of Special Scientific Interest. The Visitor Centre (tel: 01492 874151; Easter–end-Oct daily 9am–5pm) has a live camera link to enable visitors to watch local seabird colonies.

Across Llandudno's isthmus on West Shore stands the White Rabbit statue, commemorating the town's association with Lewis Carroll (alias the Rev. Charles Dodgson). He was a frequent guest of the Liddell family whose daughter, Alice, accompanied him on seashore walks and is thought to have inspired the creation of his famous storybook character. **Llandudno Museum** (Gloddaeth Street; tel: 01492 876517; www.llandudnomuseum.co.uk; Easter–Oct Tue–Sat 10.30am–1pm and 2–5pm, Sun 2.15–5pm; Nov–Easter Tue–Sat 1.30–4.30pm) has a collection of bones dating back 14,000 years, which were found in Llandudno, together with prehistoric tools, Roman items (including a tile with a footprint embedded in it) and an exhibit on wartime Llandudno.

The town's many attractions include flowery walks through Haulfre and Happy Valley gardens, a dry-ski slope and toboggan run, art exhibitions at **MOSTYN** (tel: 01492 879201; www. mostyn.org; Tue–Sun 10.30am–5pm), a stunning contemporary art gallery, and prestigious productions at the

Llandudno for Families

Llandudno is brimming with family-friendly attractions. For young ones there's a traditional Punch and Judy Show, held in summer on the North Shore Promenade. All ages should enjoy the underground tour at the Bronze Age Copper Mine on the Great Orme (especially considering the fact that some of the tunnels are thought to have been dug by children aged just 5 or 6). The whole family could also join a boat trip around the Great Orme. They take place daily from April to October (tel: 07961 561589).

Above: a Punch and Judy show captures children's attention.

(V) **Picturesque Conwy**

The battlements of Conwy Castle offer fine views – those from the North West Tower are particularly stunning, as you can see the surrounding mountains as well as Conwy's extensive town walls. The castle was a favourite subject of J.M.W. Turner, who toured North Wales and painted it several times.

Above: the view from Conwy Castle to Conwy Sands.

Venue Cymru (www.venuecymru. co.uk), a theatre and conference centre on the seafront. There are also many independent shops, selling everything from clothes to ceramics.

CONWY

Leave Llandudno on the A546, shadowing the River Conwy's eastern shore to Deganwy, and follow signs for Conwy, crossing the A55 tunnel approaches. On your left is Thomas Telford's Conwy Suspension Bridge, built in 1826 to replace the ferry, and for many years the only vehicular crossing. It is now pedestrianised with its tiny Toll House (Mar–Oct daily) restored in period style by the National Trust. Robert Stephenson's tubular railway bridge, opened 12 years later, runs alongside, carrying the main Euston to Holyhead line.

Enclosed by battlemented walls, **Conwy** ❼ is one of the best preserved medieval fortified towns in Europe, and **Conwy Castle** (tel: 01492 592358; www.cadw.wales. gov.uk; Mar–June and Sept–Oct daily 9.30am–5pm, until 6pm July and Aug, Nov–Feb daily 10am–4pm, Sun 11am–4pm; joint tickets available with Plas Mawr) dominates arrival from the east. The castle was begun in 1283, contemporary with those at Harlech and Caernarfon, under the aegis of Edward I's talented military architect, James of St George. It took just four years to build. Allow time to explore the complex and to absorb its fascinating history in the adjacent Visitor Centre.

Nearly 1 mile (1.6km) in total length, with three gateways and 21 towers, **Conwy Town Walls** have survived almost unscathed. Walking along the ramparts reveals bird's-eye views over 19th-century River Quay and the little town which boasts more

Left: a section of Conwy's Town Walls.
Right: Conwy's statue of Llewellyn the Great, who ruled most of Wales.

Above: a bridge spans the main entrance to Conwy Castle, whose towers may be climbed for spectacular views.

than 200 buildings of special architectural interest. Notable among them is **Plas Mawr** (tel: 01492 580167; www.cadw.wales.gov.uk; Apr–Sept daily 9.30am–5pm, Oct 9am–4pm), the finest Elizabethan town house in Britain. It was built for Welsh merchants, who obviously wanted to impress visitors with a display of elaborate

plasterwork. There's also an atmospheric kitchen and courtyard garden. Behind Plas Mawr is the **Royal Cambrian Academy of Art** (tel: 01492 593413; www.rcaconwy.org; Tue–Sat 11am–5pm) which exhibits the work of Welsh artists, while other attractions include **Aberconwy House** on Castle Street (tel: 01492 592246; Jan Tue–Sat 10am–5pm, Mar–June and Sept–Oct daily 11am–5pm, July–Aug daily 10am–5pm, Nov–Dec Sat–Sun noon–3pm), the town's only surviving medieval merchant's house, which is now under the care of the National Trust; and, down on the quayside, Britain's reputedly **Smallest House** (www.thesmallesthouseinbritain.co.uk; tel: 07925 049786; Apr–Oct daily 10am–4pm, until late in summer), which has just two rooms, yet was inhabited until 1900 – by a fisherman who was over 6ft (1.8m) tall.

VALE OF CONWY

Take the B5106 Trefriw road from the castle and follow it south along the pastoral Vale of Conwy. A mile (1.6km) past Ty'n-y-groes, poorly signed on the left, is a driveway to Caerhun, lowest fording point on the River Conwy since Roman times. It was guarded then by a

Above: the three-arched bridge over the River Conwy in Llanrwst, with the vine-clad National Trust property, Tu Hwnt-l'r-Bont, behind.

fort – Canovium – in whose northeast quadrant sits the tiny medieval Church of St Mary. The site is also accessible by footpath from Tal-y-cafn bridge just over a mile (1.6km) to the north.

To the north of Dolgarrog, with its large aluminium works, the B5106 passes along a broad reach of farmland before the Vale of Conwy narrows to a flat flood plain at Trefriw. The village of Trefriw clings to a steep wooded hillside and straddles the Snowdonia National Park border. It is famed for a nearby chalybeate

Go Birding

Just outside Conwy is an RSPB Reserve (Llandudno Junction; tel: 01492 584091; www.rspb.org.uk; daily 9.30am–5pm), which has a visitor centre, café and hides where you can watch for birds such as skylarks and lapwings. The site's extensive reed beds provide shelter for buntings and warblers, and you might also spot waders like the Black-tailed godwit. On Saturdays at 11am there are guided walks.

spring, which contains iron salts, and is believed to have been discovered by soldiers of the XXth Roman Legion. The Victorians, with a penchant for 'taking the waters', added a Pump Room and Bathhouse to the original ancient grotto and Trefriw Wells Spa became a major attraction.

Above Trefriw lie two lakes, Crafnant and Geirionydd (both have encircling footpaths). Their waters flow down the Afon Crafnant to **Trefriw Woollen Mill** (tel: 01492 640462; www.t-w-m.co.uk; shop, tearoom and turbine house Apr–Oct daily, Nov–Mar Mon–Sat; weaving in operation mid-Feb–mid-Dec Mon–Fri), whose water turbines power the 1950s vintage mill machinery. Here you can see the weaving of traditional Welsh tapestries and tweeds, and may also be able to try your hand at weaving on a small hand loom.

LLANRWST AND GWYDIR

Tortuous lanes to the west penetrate Gwydir Forest Park, a fascinating region of mine-scarred hills and secretive lakes. There are forest trails, picnic and car parking areas. Where

the B5106 swings left, take the right fork for Betws-y-coed. The market town of **Llanrwst** ❽ lies just across the River Conwy, spanned by the graceful 17th-century three-arched bridge, Pont Fawr, which is attributed to Inigo Jones. The village church stands on a site once occupied by a 6th-century saint's cell. The neighbouring Gwydir Chapel is said to have been built by Inigo Jones and contains part of the coffin of Llewellyn ap Iowerth (Llewellyn the Great).

Off the first bend on the B5106 stands **Gwydir Castle** (tel: 01492 641687; www.gwydircastle.co.uk), a Tudor mansion painstakingly restored following a fire in the 1920s and considered to be one of the most haunted houses in Wales. A family home (they offer bed and breakfast), the house contains a wood-panelled dining room – also attributed to Inigo Jones, who appears to have been busy in these parts – which was sold in 1921 to American press baron William Randolph Hearst and later passed to the New York Metropolitan Museum. The room was never unpacked, and in 1996 it was purchased and returned to Gwydir. Those seeking high-level adventure in the trees can

visit Tree Top Adventure (tel: 01690 710914; www.ttadventure.co.uk; daily in summer and school holidays, other times vary but booking always advised), a rope obstacle course in the trees, by the A470. Just before joining the A5 at Betws-y-coed the road crosses Pont y Pair (Bridge of the Cauldron), from which intrepid (or maybe foolhardy) youngsters plunge on hot summer days.

BETWS-Y-COED

Situated at the eastern gateway to the Snowdonia National Park, **Betws-y-coed** ❾ (pronounced Betus-er-Quoid, and meaning 'Chapel in the Wood') is built around the confluence of three rivers, the Conwy, the Llugwy and the Lledr. Popular with Victorian honeymooners, and still a great base for exploring the area, the village was put firmly on the map by the Birmingham watercolourist, David Cox. Over the years the main street of greystone cottages and hotels has sprouted a rash of craft shops, out-

Below: Betws-y-coed is the starting point for several easy walks.

door equipment stores and eating places. Several easy walks start here, particularly up to Llyn Elsi by the Jubilee Path, to forest-fringed Llyn y Parc, and along the River Llugwy to the Miners Bridge – all waymarked.

Betws has a station on the single-track **Conwy Valley Line** (www. conwyvalleyrailway.co.uk) running 27 miles/43km from Llandudno Junction to Blaenau Ffestiniog (see Tour 3, p.45) through stunning scenery. Behind the station, ignored by the crowds, sleeps the 14th-century Old Church of St Michael & All Angels, containing an effigy of Gruffydd ap Dafydd, great nephew of Llewellyn the Last, who fought in the wars of Edward III and the Black Prince. If it's closed, the key to the church can be obtained from the central complex known as Royal Oak Stables (tel: 01690 710426; daily), which houses a National Park information centre dealing with all aspects of the area.

CAPEL CURIG

From Betws-y-coed the A5 climbs slowly to Swallow Falls, a beauty spot visited since the early 19th century where the Afon Llugwy drops 30ft (9m) into a deep pool, continuing as a single foaming torrent. Less than a mile (1.6km) ahead motorists pass Ty Hyll (The Ugly House), which dates from the Middle Ages and is now the headquarters of the Snowdonia Society (tel: 01286 685498; www.snow donia-society.org.uk).

As **Capel Curig** ❿ is approached there are majestic views first of Moel Siabod (2,861ft/872m) on the left, then to the Snowdon massif and the humpback Carneddau mountains. Capel Curig's equipment shops and friendly cafés serve the needs of the year-round outdoor fraternity, as does **Plas y Brenin** (tel: 01690 720214; www.pyb.co.uk), Wales's National Mountain Sports Centre, which runs courses in everything from hillwalking and navigation to skiing and sea kayaking.

LLYN OGWEN

Five miles (8km) ahead beside Thomas Telford's London to Holyhead highway, pinched between the

Above: hiking in the countryside around Capel Curig in the northern half of the National Park.

Above: Llyn Ogwen, said to contain Excalibur, King Arthur's sword, is where the route up to the summit of Tryfan begins.

frowning Glyder and Carneddau peaks, lies **Llyn Ogwen** ⑪. Here, it is claimed, Sir Bedivere, last of Arthur's knights, cast Excalibur into the water. Llyn Ogwen is Snowdonia's shallowest lake with a mean depth of only 6ft (1.8m). Walk along the north-shore fishermen's path to appreciate the rearing bulk of Try-

Below: its convenient location adds to the Ogwen valley's popularity.

F   Carnedd Llewelyn

The highest summit in the Carneddau mountains, Carnedd Llewelyn (3,491ft/1,064m), stands a mere 69ft (21m) lower than Snowdon itself. Carneddau means 'place of stones, or cairns', but while this describes the terrain here and there, grass predominates, swathing the vast ridges and cwms.

Above: a snowy ridge on top of Carnedd Llewelyn in winter.

fan (3,002ft/915m); its proximity to the A5 and its rocky ridges leading to twin summit boulders, christened Adam and Eve, attract large numbers of walkers. A path leading south from Ogwen Cottage to Cwm Idwal follows a rugged 2-mile (3km) nature trail revealing in graphic form the region's fascinating glacial origins,

Above: the Sychnant Pass is important for its heathland of bell heather and gorse, whose colours are most impressive in August.

which attracted Charles Darwin in the 19th century. Cwm Idwal is a Site of Special Scientific Interest – Arctic plants grow here, such as moss campion, saxifrages and even an insectivorous butterwort, which traps insects in its leaves. The protected Snowdon lily also grows here – this plant, which looks more like a daisy than a lily, only grows on Snowdon and the surrounding area. From the far end of Llyn Idwal an exhilarating but very steep path climbs through the rocky cleft known as the Devil's Kitchen (Twll Du) to Llyn y Cwn and on up to the boulder-strewn Glyder tops or the smoother-contoured Y Garn. On the lake's eastern side rise the Idwal Slabs, easy-angled rock faces often used by novice climbers 'learning the ropes'.

PENRHYN CASTLE

Wriggling from the mountains' grasp, the A5 delivers motorists down the dramatic Nant Ffrancon Valley to Bethesda, named after one of the town's many slate workers' chapels. It might as readily have been 'Jerusalem' or 'Siloam'. Southwest of the town,

hemming it in, are the vast Penrhyn Slate Quarries that once employed 2,000 men and are reckoned to be the deepest in the world. Begun in Elizabethan times, they were greatly expanded on the initiative of Thomas Pennant from Liverpool, who married the Penrhyn estate heiress and became Baron Penrhyn in 1783. A short drive beyond the A55 towards Bangor will locate the National Trust's **Penrhyn Castle** ⑫ (tel: 01248 353084; www.nationaltrust.org.uk; daily Mar–Oct noon–5pm; limited tours Tue), Pennant's ostentatious, neo-Norman seat, set amidst glorious and extensive grounds. As well as fine interior craftsmanship – including a vast slate bed made for Queen Victoria – there are restored kitchens, an Industrial Railway Museum and a dolls' museum.

SYCHNANT PASS

Turn right onto the A55 coastal Expressway to Abergwyngregyn, which flanks the Carneddau foothills with wonderful views over to Anglesey and Conwy Bay. Note that a lane southeast from Abergwyngregyn leads to a Forest Enterprise car park near Bont

Newydd, start of a popular and easy 3-mile (5km) round walk to view Aber Falls. The larger cascade – Rhaedr Fawr – plunges 170ft (52m) into the boulder-choked Afon Aber.

On the A55 beyond Llanfairfechan, watch for the turn-off to Penmaen-mawr, a seaside town that has seen better days. From here, you can take the unclassified road towards Dwygy-fylchi and so to Sychnant Pass on the old coaching route between Conwy and Bangor. There are walks in both directions from the pass, with marvellous views of Puffin Island and the Vale of Conwy. Alternatively, follow the A55 back to Llandudno, and retrace your route back to Ruthin.

ⓔ Eating Out

Ruthin
On the Hill
1 Upper Clwyd Street; tel: 01824 707736; www.onthehillrestaurant.co.uk; Tue–Sat noon–2pm and 6.30–9pm.
This intimate bistro attracts plenty of local people who love its locally sourced produce and regularly changing menus. As well as braised pork, Welsh steak and an excellent range of fish dishes, there are vegetarian choices. Desserts, which are homemade, might include *bara brith* bread-and-butter pudding. ££

The Picture House
Well Street; tel: 01824 703100; www.loadsofwine.co.uk; daily noon–9pm.
A former Art Deco cinema has been turned into this restaurant/café, which offers a mix of light meals and more substantial dishes. The menu features Welsh beefburgers, surf and turf kebabs, as well as vegetarian pastas, and dishes such as Fisherman's Pie. Desserts include a selection of local cheeses. ££

Wynnstay Arms
Well Street; tel: 01824 703147; food Mon–Sat noon–2pm and 6–9pm, Sun noon–3pm.
This 16th-century coaching inn was mentioned by George Borrow in his travel account *Wild Wales*. Today, it's a gastro-pub offering locally sourced food, home-baked bread, and dishes such as pot roast lamb shank with bacon-and-basil mash. There are always vegetarian choices on the menu. ££

Llandudno
Osborne's Café
17 North Parade; tel: 01492 860330; www.osbornehouse.co.uk; daily 10.30am–9.30pm, Sun until 9pm.
Café is hardly the word to describe this opulent hotel restaurant, which offers Michelin-recommended food at very reasonable prices. There are set menus available, with mains such as local lamb shank. Osborne's also serve an afternoon tea, complete with smoked salmon, *bara brith* and scones. ££

Conwy
The Groes Inn
On B5106, 2 miles (3km) from Conwy; tel: 01492 650545; www.groesinn.com; Mar–Oct Mon–Sun and Nov–Feb Tue–Sat noon–3pm and 6–11pm
This lovely 16th-century inn on the outskirts of Conwy offers very good food featuring lots of local produce such as Welsh lamb, beef steaks and game, while amongst the desserts is home-made ice cream and Snowden pudding. ££

Llanrwst
Tu Hwnt I'r Bont
Near Inigo Jones Bridge; tel: 01492 642322; www.tuhwntirbont.co.uk; daily 10.30am–5pm.
This extraordinary 15th-century cottage is perched beside the river at Llanrwst and belongs to the National Trust. It makes a picturesque place to stop for a sandwich or a ploughman's lunch. £

Tour 2

A Tour of Anglesey

This 93-mile (150km) full-day tour takes you through the pastoral landscapes of Anglesey, which present a striking contrast to the more rugged mainland

Anglesey – Ynys Môn to the Welsh – is Britain's largest offshore island. It is joined to the mainland by two engineering marvels which span the treacherous Menai Strait: Thomas Telford's elegant suspension bridge and George Stephenson's Britannia Bridge.

Heathland, pasture and fen spread gently westwards, punctuated by wind-honed copses and villages of single-storey, pebble-dashed houses crouched against the winter winds that sweep up through St George's Channel. The island's unique character distinguishes it from the rest of Snowdonia yet you are constantly reminded of its proximity by the glorious panorama of mountains spread along the eastern horizon. Much of Anglesey's shoreline enjoys Heritage Coast or AONB (Area of

Highlights

- Llanfair Pwllgwyngyll
- Newborough Warren
- Barclodiad y Gawres
- Holy Island
- Moelfre
- Llangefni
- Beaumaris

Left: the old lighthouse on Llanddwyn Island. **Right**: Parys mountain, site of extensive copper mining.

Outstanding Natural Beauty) status, a wonderful succession of dunes and river estuaries, islands, coves and bird-haunted sea cliffs; there are glorious sandy bays too.

Anglesey's long history has woven a rich tapestry of fascinating sites, from Neolithic times through the Industrial Revolution to the 21st century. In the fishing villages and around the coast there are many associations with ship-wrecks and smuggling, while inland a profusion of wildlife co-exists with a rural economy that until the 19th cen-tury derived much of its power from windmills, the stumps of which still dot the countryside.

The A4080 and A5025 roads vir-tually encircle the island, with the A5 striking more directly northwest to its terminus at Holyhead. However, you get more intimate glimpses of coast and interior if you explore country lanes along the way – this is not a place to be rushed. A visit to Oriel Ynys Môn on the outskirts of Llangefni will give you insights into the island's distinctive culture, history and environment.

THE BRITANNIA BRIDGE

To start the tour, follow the A5122 from Bangor and join the A55 over Stephenson's **Britannia Bridge** (Pont Britannia) ❶, which was built in 1850 to carry two railway tracks, each en-closed in an iron tube. A fire in 1970 so damaged the tubes that the bridge was closed while new arches were installed and a new road deck added on top.

Turn left onto the A4080 and note on the right the 100ft (30m) Marquess

Left: Conwy suspension bridge provides views over the Conwy estuary.

🄵 Neolithic Site

Anglesey is full of Neolithic sites, and Bryn Celli Ddu, on the A4080, is one of the most important. Once a place of worship, it looks rather like a brooding hump in the land-scape. Stones surround a polygonal stone burial chamber in which were found arrowheads, mussel shells, bones and a stone bead. The site can be visited at any time.

Above: the Bryn Celli Ddu burial mound.

Above: the country house and gardens of Plas Newydd.

of Anglesey's Column. It commemorates the Marquess's heroic wounding at the Battle of Waterloo, when he exclaimed to the Duke of Wellington: 'By god sir, I've lost my leg!', to which the Duke replied: 'By god, so you have!'

PLAS NEWYDD

Watch for the A4080's left turn at **Llanfairpwllgwyngyllgogerychwyrndrobwllllantysiliogogogoch** ❷ ('St Mary's Church in the hollow of the white hazel near the rapid whirlpool and the church of St Tysilio

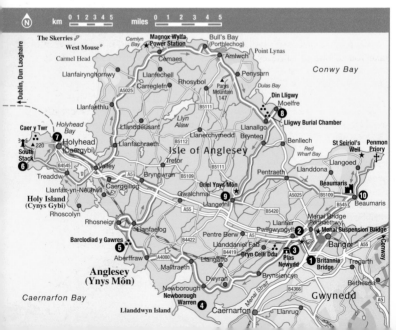

close to the red cave'). This tongue-twisting place name – generally shortened to the more manageable Llanfair PG or Llanfair Pwllgwyngyll – was probably invented in the 19th century by a local tradesman who was keen to attract tourists. It is certainly Britain's longest place name, with a railway station nameplate of national repute. A short detour off the A4080, towards the village of Llanddaniel Fab, would take you to one of Anglesey's most important Neolithic sites, Bryn Celli Ddu, a well-preserved chambered tomb *(see p.29)*.

In 1½ miles (2.5km) the road passes the National Trust's **Plas Newydd** ❸ (tel: 01248 714795; www.nationaltrust.org.uk; Apr–Nov Sat–Wed noon–4.30pm). This magnificent 18th-century neo-Gothic mansion is set in sloping parkland overlooking the Menai Strait and the Snowdonia mountains. It was the home of the first Marquess of Anglesey, who commanded the cavalry at Waterloo, but was redesigned in later years. A museum is dedicated to the Marquess, who lost his leg in the battle. Its interior pièce de résistance

is an extraordinary 58ft (18m) -wide trompe l'oeil mural painted in 1937 by Rex Whistler. Taking up a whole wall, it is an extravagant scene, encompassing the Snowdonia mountains and Portmeirion. The gardens are well worth exploring, with fine displays of rhododendrons in the spring.

From Plas Newydd, return to the A4080 and through the village of Brynsiencyn, which stands surrounded by an ancient landscape of prehistoric dolmens and burial mounds.

NEWBOROUGH WARREN

The A4080 continues to Newborough at the island's southwest tip. Since Elizabeth I's reign, marram grass has been planted to stabilise the shifting dunes here in **Newborough Warren** ❹. Before 1930, when afforestation began, the grass was woven into mats and brushes while the warren's rabbit population provided valuable protein for the local diet. A forestry toll road runs down to Llanddwyn Bay's 4-mile (6.5km) -long beach, and there are walks in the 2,000-acre (800-hectare) Newborough Forest.

Above: Newborough Warren was created when storms carpeted the farming region with a blanket of sand; the dunes are now stabilised by marram grass.

The area has been designated a National Nature Reserve and is extremely rich in wildlife. Plants include orchids and butterworts, skylarks can often be heard, and there is a multitude of invertebrates, including the medicinal leech. In winter, the mudflats become home to a variety of birds including pintail, wigeon and redshank. Near Newborough Warren is a finger of land known as Llanddwyn Island. It is associated with St Dwynwen, a 5th-century saint who is the Welsh patron saint of lovers. Her feast day is 25 January.

For almost 30 years before his death in 1979 the wildlife artist Charles Tunnicliffe lived at Malltraeth, recording the island's landscapes and especially its birds. His work is represented in Oriel Ynys Môn at Llangefni.

ABERFFRAW TO HOLY ISLAND

Immense sandhills separate Aberffraw's beach from road and village as the route proceeds along the A4080. Here was an ancient seat of the powerful Princes of Gwynedd and their main Court (Llys) up to the 13th century. Nothing remains of the original timber buildings.

An alternative A4080 loop route a little further north, leads to Rhosneigr (from Rhos y Neidr, 'Moor of the Adder'), perched on a little rocky promontory at the mouth of the Afon Crigyll. Its demure whitewashed cottages belie a darker past when a gang of wreckers lured ships onto this rugged shore. They were finally caught and hanged at Beau-

---

ⓕ Druids' Last Stand

The Druids were Celtic religious leaders who had a powerful base on Anglesey. They are said to have preached immortality through rebirth and to occasionally have made human sacrifices. Caesar wrote of them as a 'privileged class', and they provided strong opposition to the Roman forces. The Romans gradually pushed them out of mainland Wales, until they were isolated on Anglesey and finally massacred around AD 61.

maris in 1741 and later became the subject of a local ballad.

If you're interested in Anglesey's Neolithic past, then stop at Llanfaelog, at the Wayside Stores to visit **Barclodiad y Gawres** ❺ (www.cadw.wales.gov.uk; daily 10am–4pm, burial chamber by appointment Apr–Oct Sat–Sun noon–4pm). This is possibly the most important Neolithic site in Wales, and sits a mile (1.6km) away, northwest of Aberffraw on the Anglesey Coastal Path. It is reached by a locked gate; staff at the stores have a key and can accompany you. Barclodiad y Gawres, which is managed by Cadw (the Welsh Assembly's historic environment division), is a fine example of a passage grave. It was built around 3000 BC and features stones that have been decorated with spirals and swirls.

Fork left just under half a mile (500m) northeast of Llanfaelog, joining the A5 just before Bryngwran for Holyhead. At Caergeiliog planespotters can take the lane south to the railway bridge at Llanfair-yn-Neubwll, or further to Carnau, there to watch the comings and goings at

RAF Valley with its training school for jet pilots and air-sea rescue station.

HOLY ISLAND

A detour out to Holy Island (Ynys Gybi) is recommended. This small island just off Anglesey (they're connected by a bridge) got its name as it was settled in the 6th century by a monk, St Cybi, a cousin of St David. The B4545 to Treaddur Bay gives way to tortuous lanes over to **South Stack** ❻, a rocky islet reached by pedestrian bridge at the bottom of 350 steps. Over 4,000 pairs of seabirds, including puffins, guillemots, razorbills and fulmars, breed in this RSPB reserve (tel: 01407 762100; www.rspb.org.uk) each spring and early summer, observable from the Ellin's Tower Visitor Centre (Easter–Sept daily 10am–5pm). You may also spot ravens and peregrines, while the heathland is important for the chough. Choughs are the rarest type of crow in the UK, and South Stack has several breeding pairs.

The nearby Gogarth Bay sea cliffs are a popular rock-climbing venue and there are also clifftop walks to North

Below: lighthouse on South Stack, an important seabird breeding location.

Above: Parys Mountain's copper mine was the world's largest throughout the 18th and 19th centuries.

Stack. At 722ft (220m), **Holyhead Mountain** is Anglesey's highest ground by far, with views to match. Hut circles and the large Caer y Twr, an Iron Age hillfort, indicate mankind's occupation of this exposed peninsula spanning many centuries.

HOLYHEAD

Holyhead ❼ (Caergybi) is Anglesey's largest town and an important sea port for services to Dublin and Dun Laoghaire. The arrival of Telford's road from London in 1821, marked by a triumphal Doric arch, and the railway shortly afterwards, transformed the harbour's fortunes. A huge breakwater almost 2 miles (3km) long was built (it took 30 years) to protect the anchorage's 700 acres (280 hectares) from northwesterly gales. In the centre of the town is **St Cybi's church**, founded by the saint in an abandoned Roman fortress. The church pews have pagan Green Men carved on the ends, and there are Pre-Raphaelite stained-glass windows by William Morris and Edward Burne-Jones.

North from Holyhead, lanes branch out from the A5025 towards the shore of Holyhead Bay where coves and low cliffs alternate towards Carmel Head. Offshore lie the Skerries and West Mouse islands, hazards in the days of sail when anxious Liverpool shipowners awaited news of their vessels.

NORTH COAST

Anglesey's north coast is closely shadowed by roads, but there is a fine stretch of coastal footpath too, especially between Cemaes and Amlwch. Car parks at both ends of Cemlyn Bay's great shingle bank and lagoon allow access for walking and for viewing seabirds. Wales' only nuclear power station, the Magnox Wylfa Power Station, can be seen west of Cemlyn Bay. Before Amlwch's ascendancy in the late 18th century, Cemaes and Porthlechog (Bull's Bay) were centres for fishing, coastal trade and smuggling. **Amlwch** itself became a boom town when top-grade copper ore was discovered in nearby Parys Mountain during 1768. The ore was dug in open-cast workings and within 30 years the population had exploded to 6,000. Competition from cheaper American and African copper eventually ended the UK boom. The 'moonscape' of Parys Mountain, along with

Llyn Alaw, Anglesey's largest lake, lies just to the south.

MOELFRE

Extensive sands characterise Anglesey's sheltered eastern coast, particularly bordering Dulas, Lligwy and Red Wharf bays; in between, however, treacherous rocks have caused many a shipwreck. It was north of Moelfre in October 1859 that the steam clipper *Royal Charter*, inward bound from the Australian goldfields, foundered in huge seas with the loss of over 450 lives and an estimated £370,000 of prospectors' gold. Visit **Moelfre** ❽ where its **Seawatch Centre** (tel: 01248 410300; daily Feb–Dec 10.30am–4.30pm), run by the Royal National Lifeboat Institution, gives an insight into the maritime heritage of the area. Outside is a bronze statue of Richard 'Dic' Evans, a member of the Moelfre lifeboat team, who won two gold medals for his bravery. Not far from Moelfre (signposted from the roundabout on the A5025 southwest of the village) is Lligwy, site of **Din Lligwy**, the remains of a 1st-century farmstead probably settled during the Roman occupation. One of the most impressive ancient sites in Britain, it may have been the home of a Celtic chieftain; some buildings still possess substantial walls with doorposts and traces of drainage systems across the floor. Nearby is **Lligwy burial chamber**, a late Neolithic tomb that contained the remains of around 30 individuals. The tomb would originally have been covered with earth. In a field is the ruined chapel **Capel Lligwy**, which dates back to the 12th century. For unrivalled panoramic views, climb to the little 584ft (178m) summit of Mynydd Bodafon, reached up a lane off the A5025.

LLANGEFNI

Half a mile (0.8km) south of the Moelfre roundabout, turn right onto the B5110. The administrative capital of Anglesey and its principal market town, **Llangefni** ❾ epitomises the island's rural Welsh heart. Although the traditional cattle market has moved out of the town centre, The Square, near the Bull Hotel, remains a constantly bustling focal point. On the town's outskirts along the B5111 to the north stands **Oriel Ynys Môn** (tel: 01248 724444; www.kyffinwilliams.info; daily 10.30am–5pm), which houses an excellent permanent exhibition featuring Anglesey's history, culture and environment. There are artefacts from the wrecked *Royal Charter*, and Neolithic items ranging from flints to a gold ring. Part of the space is devoted to the work of the wildlife artist Charles Tunnicliffe, and there is also a Kyffin Williams gallery featuring the eponymous artist's work.

Ⓖ A Puffin Cruise

Puffin Island Cruises (tel: 01248 810746) run 1-hour boat trips from Beaumaris Pier around Puffin Island, also known as Seiriol's Island after the small monastic community established here by St Seiriol. The island provides a home to seabirds such as puffins and razorbills. You may also spot some seals on the trip.

Above: uninhabited Puffin Island is the site of a protected seabird colony.

Above: the interior of Beaumaris Gaol.

BEAUMARIS

Follow the B5109 via Pentraeth to **Beaumaris** ❿ (from 'beau maris', Norman-French for 'beautiful marsh'). Last in Edward I's chain of coastal fortresses against the Welsh, **Beaumaris Castle** (tel: 01248 810361; www.cadw.wales.gov.uk; Mar–June and Sept–Oct daily 9.30am–5pm, July–Aug until 6pm, Nov–Feb Mon–Sat 10am–4pm, Sun 11am–4pm) dates back to 1295 and is Britain's most technically perfect medieval castle, with concentric rings of defensive walls inside a deep moat; there was even a jetty that enabled provisioning to take place from the sea. It was designed by Edward I's architect Master James of St George. It was certainly intended to repel all attackers, with inner walls up to 16ft (4.8m) thick, as well as 'murder holes' and arrow slits. The castle last saw action in 1646, during the English Civil War. Opposite stands the 17th-century **Courthouse** (tel: 01248 811691; Apr–Sept

Right: the high street in Beaumaris, a major yachting centre.

Sat–Thur 10.30am–5pm), which was last used as a court in 1971. Visitors can stand in the dock, and find out about past trials on Anglesey.

Behind the Parish Church to the west you will find the 19th-century **Gaol** (tel: 01248 810921; hours as Courthouse; joint tickets available). This Victorian structure, built by the man who designed the Hansom cab, provides a grim reminder of prison life in earlier times. The gaol contains an original tread wheel (used as punishment), and a gibbet. Visitors can see the cells, including the condemned cell, and even handle chains that were used to shackle the unfortunate prisoners.

PENMON PRIORY

To visit **Penmon Priory** ruins and St Seiriol's Well, take the B5109 north and follow signs along the narrow access lanes. The original priory, founded here and on neighbouring Priestholm (Puffin Island) in the 6th century by the hermit St Seiriol, was burnt down by the Danes. The present Penmon Church, containing some splendid Norman features, dates from the

12th century, the associated monastic buildings from the 13th to the 16th centuries. East of the priory, a massive dovecote was built around 1600 to house up to 1,000 pigeons destined for the table of local landowner Sir Richard Bulkeley. It is near St Seiriol's Well, which was once said to have had healing properties.

The A545 leads along the shoreline of the Menai Strait to Menai Bridge where **Thomas Telford's Suspension Bridge** is crossed. Having overcome the greatest challenge on his London to Holyhead turnpike, Telford himself drove home the final suspension chain link on the world's first large-scale iron bridge of this design, which opened in 1826.

Above: Penmon Church contains two crosses from the medieval monastery.

Ⓔ Eating Out

Rhoscolyn
The White Eagle
Rhoscolyn; tel: 01407 860267; www.white-eagle.co.uk; food served Mon–Fri noon–2.30pm and 6–9pm; Sat until 9pm, Sun until 8.30pm.
You get sea views from this popular pub which offers old favourites such as fish and chips, as well as steaks, Welsh lamb, plus good vegetarian options. Desserts include a satisfying sticky-toffee pudding. ££

Beaumaris
The Bulls Head Inn
Castle Street; tel: 01248 810329; www.bullsheadinn.co.uk; restaurant Tue–Thur 7–9.30pm, Fri–Sat 6.30–9.30pm; brasserie daily noon–2pm and 6–9pm.
This popular inn serves modern British food, with lots of local produce. Restaurant starters might include spiced black bream and bacon, with mains like Welsh beef fillet, and a warmed dark beer cake for dessert. The less formal brasserie offers classics like steak and chips, fish tagine or Welsh Cheddar macaroni. If you're eating in the brasserie

you're advised to arrive early, as they don't take bookings. ££–£££

Nr Beaumaris
The Ship Inn
Red Wharf Bay, off A5025; tel: 01248 852568; www.shipinnredwharfbay.co.uk; daily lunch and dinner.
This traditional coastal pub offers plenty of fresh fish, as well as dishes such as chicken with wild mushrooms, or lamb shank. There's a good choice of sandwiches at lunch time, and a children's menu. The pub has a beer garden for fine days. £

Nr Holyhead
The Lobster Pot
Church Bay; tel: 01407 730241; www.thelobsterpotrestaurant.co.uk; Feb–Nov Tue–Sun lunch and dinner, limited winter opening hours.
A former traditional longhouse, this restaurant has dark beams and is simply furnished. As the name suggests, it specialises in local seafood, and the menu features oysters, lobsters and crabs. Some meat dishes and vegetarian options. £££

Bards and Legends

The Welsh tradition of story telling is a strong one, continuing down through generations from its origins in the Dark Ages to the modern period

MONSTERS AND DRAGONS

The most important collection of medieval tales – the four branches of the Mabinogion – is contained in two texts from around the mid-14th century: the White Book of Rhydderch and the Red Book of Hergest. Although these tales were written down around the 13th century, they are considered to be of much earlier origin. They weren't translated into English until the 19th century when their translator, Lady Charlotte Guest, gave them their collective title which means 'Tales of Youth'. Amongst the characters featured is King Arthur,

together with his noble knights. Monsters and dragons also feature widely in North Wales' folklore. The red dragon, now on the Welsh national flag, appears in the Mabinogion and also a later legend in which two dragons – one red, one white – sleep beneath Dinys Emrys in Snowdonia: the red dragon symbolised the Celts; the white, the Saxons. The dragons fought and the red was the victor. Henry Tudor, on his way to Bosworth, flew a flag emblazoned with a dragon.

Another legend features the *afanc* of Glaslyn, whose supernatural pow-

to the oxen and dragged through the parish of Dolwyddelan. Over the shoulder between Moel Siabod and Cribau – Bwlch Rhiw-yr-Ychain (Pass of the Oxen's Slope) – they went, one ox losing an eye with the effort, which shed tears to form Pwll Llygad yr Ych (Pool of the Ox's Eye). Struggling up into Cwm Dyli, past Llyn Llydaw, the exhausted team finally released the *afanc* into the deep waters of Llyn Ffynnon Las (Lake of the Blue Fountain), now called Glaslyn. And there he dwells to this day.

THE EISTEDDFOD

The medieval Welsh story teller (*y cyfarwydd* – the learned one), like the poet, enjoyed a high social status as court entertainer. He needed a powerful memory and expert narrative techniques to re-create tales and folklore at each performance. The Eisteddfod ('gathering') dates back to meetings between Celtic bards, when they would compete for positions in court and in wealthy households. The first recorded bardic contest was that of 1176, convened at Cardigan castle by Rhys ap Gruffydd. It was proclaimed a year and a day in advance (a custom still observed) to ensure high standards; miniature silver chains were presented as prizes for poetry and music. In the 19th century the tradition, which had begun to die out, was revived with an internationally significant Eisteddfod held in Carmarthen. In 1880 the National Eisteddfod of Wales (tickets tel: 0845 4090 800; www.eisteddfod.org.uk) was formed to stage an annual festival to promote high cultural standards, and help to safeguard the Welsh language. The festival is held alternately in North and South Wales during the first week of August and is a traditional neo-druidic ceremony, occurring within a specially laid-out Gorsedd Circle of Stones to the accompaniment of harp music. It is Europe's largest arts and music festival.

ers were upsetting people in the Vale of Conwy, causing disastrous floods, ruining crops and drowning livestock. It lived in a Beaver Pool near Betws-y-coed. When elders decided to remove it to some other distant lake, they forged strong iron chains and got two mighty oxen ready. A damsel lured the *afanc* from its underwater lair (it evidently had a predilection for beautiful maidens), whereupon it was tethered

Above: Druidic ceremony during National Eisteddfod; **Top Left**: Welsh flag. **Centre Left**: appointment of a new Archdruid, 1959. **Left**: playing the tin whistle at an international Eisteddfod in Llangollen.

Tour 3

Beddgelert and Porthmadog

At 81 miles (130km) this tour takes you to some of the best-known spots in Snowdonia, passing sights of great scenic beauty, industrial heritage and rich history

Throughout Snowdonia one finds echoes of those intrepid Victorians who flocked to the region in a search for scenery that embodied notions of the romantic and picturesque. The Napoleonic Wars in Europe meant that they were unable to embark on the Grand Tour, which took them over the dramatic mountains of the Alps to great cities such as Florence and Rome. And so, seeking equivalent drama at home, they went to the Highlands of Scotland, the Lake District and North Wales, making resorts out of sleepy hamlets and establishing a trend for enjoying the great outdoors. Angling, walking, climbing, sketching or simply admiring the scenery all drew visitors to this part of Wales, among them William

Highlights

- Beddgelert
- Porthmadog
- Ffestiniog Railway
- Blaenau Ffestiniog and Slate Caverns
- Dolwyddelan Castle
- Ty Mawr Wybrnant

Wordsworth, Sir Walter Scott and the painter J.M.W. Turner. This popularisation spurred the development of such places as Betws-y-coed, Capel Curig, Beddgelert and Dolwyddelan.

The less well-off local population still had to work for a living, often in arduous conditions. Copper mining, agriculture and fishing continued to

Above: a wood craft shop in Beddgelert. **Left**: view of the Snowdon range from Porthmadog.

employ labour as they had for centuries, but it was the building trade's insatiable appetite for roofing slate that brought about the greatest changes and opportunities. The hills around Blaenau Ffestiniog and many other locations were devastated by quarrying, their slate transported by narrow-gauge railway to quaysides on the coast, such as those at Porthmadog.

BETWS-Y-COED

This tour starts in **Betws-y-coed ❶** where the A5 climbs past Swallow Falls to reach the straggling village of Capel Curig (see *Tour 1, p.24*). Take the A4086 past Plas y Brenin, Wales's National Mountain Sports Centre, which runs courses in an enormous variety of outdoor disciplines, and enjoy a classic view of Snowdon seen across the waters of Llynnau Mymbyr. The Nantygwryd valley forms a broad trench between Moel Siabod (2,861ft/872m) and the Glyder range, whose rugged slopes fill northern views right along to the Pen y Gwryd junction. Up to the right lies Pen-y-Pass, starting point for two popular paths up Snowdon and, beyond, the Llanberis Pass (see *Tour 4, p.56*).

LLYN GWYNANT

Keep straight on along the A498 and in a mile (1.6km) or so there are lay-bys from which to admire the Snowdon massif from the east. Cwm Dyli, a deep U-shaped hollow containing hydro-electric pipelines, was scoured out by an Ice Age glacier which then turned abruptly southwest to form the valley Nantgwynant. The road coils narrowly downhill to beautiful, shingle-beached Llyn Gwynant. At its southern end hills encroach, forming a glen connecting with Llyn Dinas. Strangely reminiscent of a Chinese landscape painting, this area was chosen in 1958 as a location for filming *Inn of the Sixth Happiness*. Unseen up to the left, the Moelwyn hills cradle myriad small lakes, but they are quite remote and only accessible on foot.

❻ Male Voice Choirs

Choral music came to Wales with non conformity – and chapels put great emphasis on hymn singing. But it was industrialisation that brought male voice choirs, which in Victorian times could be 150 strong. The distinctive sound is less frequently heard today, but there are still choirs in North Wales and visitors are usually welcome to attend rehearsals. Just ask the local tourist office for details.

Above: the best choirs compete at the National Eisteddfod.

SYGUN COPPER MINE

Yr Aran (2,451ft/747m) rears a shapely head to the north and the road reaches **Sygun Copper Mine** ❷ (tel: 01766 890595; www.sygun coppermine.co.uk; daily end Mar–Oct 9.30am–5pm, Nov–Mar until 4pm). Begun around 1830 but never a commercial success owing to the low-grade ore, Sygun mine was abandoned in 1903. Extensively restored since then, you can take a self-guided audio tour of the tunnels and chambers, learn about the lives of the miners who worked here and see veins of copper ore. The mine is characterised by its green stalactites and stalagmites. There's also a small museum, containing an array of oddities like dinosaur eggs, Stone Age coins and a mammoth tooth.

BEDDGELERT

There are scenic paths over to Cwm Bychan and the Pass of Aberglaslyn, while an unclassified mountain road with picnic areas runs from Pont Bethania through Nantmor. However, the main road itself goes through **Beddgelert** ❸, which is surely the prettiest village in North Wales. Its buildings are clustered around the confluence of the Glaslyn and Colwyn rivers beneath the dominant presence of Moel Hebog (2,569ft/783m). Alfred Bestall, who created the comic character Rupert Bear for the *Daily Express* newspaper, spent schoolboy holidays here and later purchased a house in the village called Penlan; many of the scenes pictured in the comic strip were inspired by the scenery at Beddgelert. Bestall died in 1986.

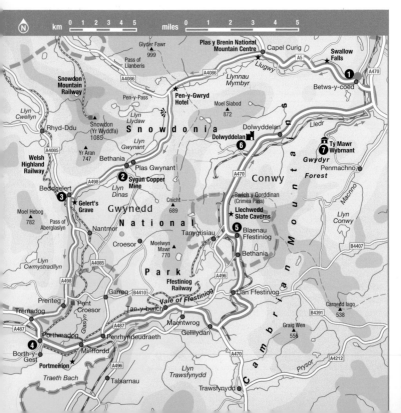

Above: incredibly scenic Beddgelert, whose tourist board runs guided walks in the valley during several weeks in summer.

Beddgelert has been immortalised by the apocryphal legend of Gelert, Llewellyn the Great's faithful hound – *bedd* means grave in Welsh. **Gelert's Grave** can be seen just to the south of the village, under a tree in a meadow by the Afon Glaslyn. However, it's more likely that the grave referred to is not that of the dog, but that of Celert, a 6th-century Celtic saint. St Mary's Church in the village has 6th-century origins. The religious community eventually established an Augustinian priory here, but it was destroyed by fire in the 13th century. Although restored, it then suffered after the Dissolution of the monasteries in Henry VIII's reign, and today the church is all that is left.

Beddgelert, which boasts a great ice-cream shop, makes an excellent base for exploring Snowdonia and is

ⓕ The Story of Gelert

Gelert was Prince Llewellyn's dog. Legend has it that the prince left the dog to guard his little son, but when he returned he discovered the bed empty and covered in blood – with the child missing. Llewellyn assumed Gelert had killed the little boy and he murdered the faithful dog – only to discover the child lying safe nearby, beside the body of a dead wolf which Gelert had bravely killed. However, it's thought that an enterprising publican made up the tale to attract visitors in the 18th century. It seemed to work.

Above: the grave can be found by following a riverside footpath.

a starting point for walks of all kinds, from easy rambles to mountain hikes. You can also hire bikes in the village and explore the surrounding forest tracks. Beddgelert is a stop on the marvellous Welsh Highland Railway, a restored steam railway that runs from Caernarfon (see *Tour 4, p.51*).

TREMADOG

Having left Beddgelert, keep right at the Pass of Aberglaslyn, still on the A498. The route goes through woods with tantalising views of Tremadog Bay, then clings to the western edge of reclaimed marshland on the Afon Glaslyn's flood plain, before reaching Tremadog, best known for its road-side rock-climbing crags and the near-by café. T.E. Lawrence (Lawrence of Arabia) was born in the village which was developed as a staging post in the early 19th century by William Madocks, Member of Parliament for Boston, Lincolnshire. It formed part of his ambitious, though ultimately unsuccessful, scheme to establish a new mail route to Ireland using Porth Dinllaen on the north coast of the Lleyn Peninsula (see *Tour 5, p.62*). **Tremadog** was a carefully planned settlement, and had one of the first woollen mills in Wales. The town's chapel is unusual, built in the style

Above: Porthmadog's marina is one of Wales' most popular mooring areas.

of a Greek temple, while St Mary's Church was built in the 19th century in neo-Gothic style.

PORTHMADOG

Turn left onto the A487 and into **Porthmadog ❹**. These days Porthmadog is a bustling holiday centre for outdoor activities, and a real hub for steam railway fans, but in times past its prosperity was dependent on the slate industry. From its quaysides, ships loaded with Ffestiniog slate, brought down by narrow-gauge rail-

Below: Tremadog Bay is an inlet of Cardigan Bay, and has several seaside resorts situated on its shores.

Above: the steam-powered, narrow-gauge Ffestiniog train allows you to see swathes of North Wales that are inaccessible by road.

way from the great quarries around Blaenau Ffestiniog, set sail for destinations worldwide. The small but interesting **Porthmadog Maritime Museum** (www.porthmadogmaritime museum.org.uk; Apr–Oct Tue–Thur and Sat–Sun noon–4pm), located in the last remaining slate shed on the harbour, charts the seafaring history of the town.

A Local Brew

If you'd like to pick up some traditionally brewed local beers, then call in to the Purple Moose Brewery in Porthmadog (Madoc Street; tel: 01766 515571; www.purplemoose. co.uk). As well as a shop, they also offer brewery tours (call beforehand to arrange) which show you the brewing process from start to finish. Tours end with a tasting.

Porthmadog itself was designed by William Madocks. A path from the harbour leads along to neighbouring Borth-y-Gest, another erstwhile slate port with a curving quay backed by cottages.

The world-renowned narrow-gauge, steam **Ffestiniog Railway** (tel: 01766 516000; www.festrail. co.uk; daily throughout the high season but consult timetable) began life in 1832, conveying industrial slate from the great Ffestiniog quarries to Porthmadog quay. It ceased operating in 1946, but was enthusiastically rescued from oblivion in 1954, and since then has enjoyed burgeoning popularity. The full 13½-mile (22km) journey takes an hour each way and provides spectacular views from the carriage windows, especially outside the season of full tree foliage. It goes from sea level at Porthmadog and climbs 700ft (213m) into the mountains. Connections with the **Conwy Valley Line** (www.conwy.gov.uk/cvr) at Blaenau Ffestiniog open up numerous travel permutations, as the 27-mile (43km) line goes to Betws-y-coed

Above: choose from a guided tramway or deep mine tour at the Llechwedd Slate Caverns at Blaenau Ffestiniog.

and then Llandudno. At Porthmadog, the Ffestiniog Railway connects with the **Welsh Highland Railway** (tel: 01766 513402; www.whr.co.uk; Easter–Oct daily but consult timetable). This runs for 25 miles (40km) to Caernarfon. The route goes by the brooding presence of Snowdon, then into Beddgelert before its terminus at Caernarfon, and the majority of trains are steam hauled.

MAENTWROG

Cheek by jowl with the railway, the road crosses the mile-long (1.6km) embankment across the Glaslyn estuary known as **The Cob** (small toll), a famous Madocks creation behind which some 7,000 acres (2,800 hectares) were reclaimed from the sea. If visibility is good there are stunning mountain views over the estuary. The shapeliest cone is Cnicht (2,261ft/689m), the so-called 'Welsh Matterhorn'. In about a mile (1.6km), Minffordd is reached where the Ffestiniog and main Cambrian Coast line between Pwllheli and Aberystwyth intersect, each with a station allowing

interchange. Beyond Penrhyndeudraeth (headquarters of the Snowdonia National Park) the A487 follows the Afon Dwyryd to Tan-y-bwlch in the lovely Vale of Ffestiniog. Once over the river it joins the A496 near the pretty village of **Maentwrog**, named after a large stone in the churchyard said to have been thrown there from the hills above by the giant Twrog. The novelist Thomas Love Peacock, a friend of the poet Shelley, spent much time here, eventually marrying the local rector's daughter. Another literary association involves the great English poet Gerard Manley Hopkins who found inspiration for his work during a visit here. Follow the road, then bear north on the A470 to Blaenau Ffestiniog.

BLAENAU FFESTINIOG

When the National Park was designated in 1952, **Blaenau Ffestiniog** ❺ and neighbouring Tanygrisiau were excluded: national park criteria were hardly met, it was argued, by an area of decaying slate tips, disused quarries and high local unemployment requiring an influx of alternative industries. It still rains for over 100 days each year in Blaenau Ffestiniog and by traditional yardsticks the surroundings remain bleak, yet this has become part of Blaenau's very appeal. The landscape of brooding grey slate possesses a sense of drama that you find in few places in the UK. Since the early days public perceptions have changed, particularly in regard to industrial archaeology, and there is even talk now that the area be included in the National Park. Tourism has certainly transformed Blaenau's fortunes. Witness, for example, the success of the **Llechwedd Slate Caverns** (tel: 01766 830306; www.

llechwedd-slate-caverns.co.uk; daily 9.30am–5.30pm, last tour 4.30pm), a highly educational and absorbing tourist attraction. There are two tours available. The first, a guided tour a third of a mile (0.5km) into the side of the mountain on a tramway, gives you an insight into the lives of the men who worked in these mines. The tour ends at the Victorian slate mill, where slates were split before being transported. The second is a deep mine tour, in which you descend 150ft (45m) underground, then follow a virtual guide to walk through tunnels and caverns. It is fascinating to note that because they only worked by candlelight, the miners

Ⓕ Great Welsh Railways

Wales is a great destination for anyone who loves scenic railway journeys. The country industrialised extremely early and rail links were built to carry goods quickly to ports and markets. When the industries declined, so did the railways. However, enthusiastic volunteers have restored many of these routes into tourist lines, frequently using vintage steam locomotives. As well as the well-known Ffestiniog and Welsh Highland railways, there is the Bala Lake Railway (www.bala-lake-railway.co.uk) which runs for 9 miles/14km along Lake Bala from Llanuwchllyn, and the Llanberis Lake Railway (www.lake-railway.co.uk), a narrow-gauge steam railway from Gilfach Ddu to Lake Padarn and back. To the east of the Snowdonia National Park is the Llangollen Railway (www.llangollen-railway.co.uk), which runs from Llangollen to Carrog, while in the west is the coastal Fairbourne to Barmouth steam railway (www.fairbournerailway.com).

Above: riding the Bala Lake Railway takes around one hour.

Above: Dolwyddelan Castle. The fairly scarce ruins are compensated for by the view from the castle's keep.

never actually saw the huge caverns they created. There is also a Victorian village (open Apr–Sept), which grew up to serve the mining community. The last residents left in the 1970s. Restored buildings include the sweet shop and village blacksmith's workshop. It is an excellent place to bring children. There's also a working pub, The Miners' Arms.

At Tanygrisiau there are walks from the road-end up to Llyn Cwmorthin in a valley strewn with evocative relics from a bygone era of intensive slate working. A derelict chapel, ruined workers' cottages and abandoned slate sheds crouch beneath the brooding Moelwyn hills whose highest point – Moelwyn Mawr (2,526ft/770m) – overlooks the Stwlan Dam.

DOLWYDDELAN CASTLE

The A470 climbs determinedly north to the Crimea Pass at 1,263ft (385m) above sea level. Opinion is divided as to whether it was named after the mid 19th-century war or a pub that once stood on the site of the present car park at the top. Af-

ter locals repeatedly complained of rowdiness in 1910 the pub was demolished with true non conformist vindictiveness.

Coming down off the pass facing vast views ahead, the road descends as a long dramatic sweep into the wooded valley of the Afon Lledr. It crosses the railway line, which has not long since emerged from a 2-mile (3km) -long tunnel, to reach **Dolwyddelan Castle** ❻ (tel: 01690 750366; www. cadw.wales.gov.uk; Oct–Mar Mon–Sat 10am–4pm, Sun 11.30am–4pm, Apr–Sept Mon-Sat 10am–5pm, Sun 11.30am–4pm). Situated on a knoll on the southern slopes of Moel Siabod, a little way from the roadside car park along a good path, the castle stands over the route from the Conwy and Lledr valleys over to Dyffryn Maentwrog – broadly the way just followed. It was built by the Welsh in the late 12th century, but its upper parts are a 19th-century reconstruction. Tradition has it that Llewellyn the Great was born here, though this is unlikely – it is more likely that he built it. The castle was besieged and fell to the in-

TY MAWR WYBRNANT

With numerous twists and turns the A470 drops eastwards towards the confluence of the Lledr and Machno rivers in woodland that becomes outstandingly beautiful when it dons its autumnal foliage. South from the A470, but only accessible on very narrow lanes, will be found the National Trust's **Ty Mawr Wybrnant** ❼ (tel: 01690 760213; www.nationaltrust.org. uk; Apr–Oct Thur–Sun noon–5pm), a remote 16th-century farmhouse and birthplace of William Morgan who first translated the Bible into Welsh.

This was the result of an Act of Parliament in Elizabeth I's reign, which allowed translation into Welsh because so many people in Wales at that time did not understand English. In 1588 the first copies of the Welsh Bible were printed.

A minor road from Penmachno offers a pleasant return to Betws-y-coed. The Penmachno village itself sits in an unspoilt valley and is well known for its weaving tradition.

vading English in January 1283, though subsequently in the late 15th century it was reoccupied by Maredudd ab Ieuan, a descendant of the Prince of Powys who led Welsh resistance against Henry I in the 13th century. In Dolwyddelan village, south of the main road, stands the delightful little 16th-century Old Church.

Ⓔ Eating Out

Betws-y-coed

Alpine Coffee Shop
Station Approach; tel: 01690 710747; www.alpinecoffeeshop.net; Mon–Fri 8.30am–5.30pm, Sat–Sun 8am–5.30pm.
This welcoming café at Betws-y-coed railway station offers a varied menu featuring all-day breakfasts, Mexican wraps and Mediterranean boards, as well as mouthwatering afternoon teas. The coffee is excellent, too. There are plenty of vegetarian, vegan and gluten-free options and all dishes are palm-oil free. Dogs are welcome and invited to enjoy the local sausages! £

Bridge 1815 Brasserie
Waterloo Hotel; tel: 01690 710411; www.waterloo-hotel.info; daily lunch and dinner.

This hotel bistro serves modern British dishes. During the day sandwiches and light meals are available, while in the evening guests can enjoy starters such as Welsh goats' cheese and beetroot cheesecake, steaks and fish dishes, and a range of desserts. Vegetarian choices might include wild mushroom tart. ££

Ty Gwyn
By Waterloo Bridge; tel: 01690 710383; www.tygwynhotel.co.uk; daily lunch and dinner.
This very popular inn serves a wide range of bar meals, and also has a restaurant. Dishes range from Powys fillet steak or suckling pig to Aberdaron lobster. Desserts might include honeycomb, chocolate and ginger cheesecake. ££

Tour 4

Snowdon from Caernarfon

This 38-mile (62km) full day's tour will take you to Mount Snowdon itself, the highest peak in Wales, before heading down to the coast and the ancient town of Caernarfon

No visit to Snowdonia is complete without seeing Yr Wyddfa (Snowdon's Welsh name) at close quarters. Rising to 3,560ft (1,085m), it is the highest peak in England and Wales and one that offers itself generously to all who seek to explore its great crags and cwms (valleys).

There are six main tracks to the summit, while the less mobile may scale the heights by means of the famous Snowdon Mountain Railway. Needless to say, inexperienced hillwalkers should climb up only in good weather and should wear appropriate clothing.

Yr Wyddfa means 'tomb' or 'monument', a reference to the burial of the legendary Rhita Gawr, an ogre with a predilection for slaying kings, who was himself killed at the summit by King

Highlights

- Caernarfon Castle
- Llanberis
- Snowdon Mountain Railway
- National Slate Museum
- Dolbadarn Castle
- The Pass of Llanberis

Arthur. Botanist Thomas Johnson wrote the first account of an ascent in 1639, but it was Thomas Pennant's published tours that popularised the mountain in the late 18th century, and another Thomas – Telford – whose London to Holyhead road provided the accessibility. By the 1830s, guiding was already proving profitable, often using horses to convey visitors by the easier Llanberis

Track. As early as 1854, on his famous tour of Wales, George Borrow found the track 'thronged with tourists as far as the eye could reach…' Accommodation and refreshments became available in wooden huts clustered around the huge summit cairn and operated by competing hotels in the valley. When the first train service began in 1896, a new era of summit building started, culminating in the demolition of the by-then squalid huts. The 1930s saw construction of a complex designed by Clough Williams-Ellis, creator of the Portmeirion Italianate village. Trains to the summit terminate at the Hafod Eryri visitor centre (see p.57).

CAERNARFON

This drive starts down at sea level, in what is surely the most Welsh of towns; **Caernarfon ❶**. Caernarfon is a busy holiday town, market and administrative centre. Its old streets and alleyways, its Georgian houses around The Square and its historic inns all exude flavours from a diverse past, and it is also the starting point

for the vintage Welsh Highland Railway line (see *Tour 3, p.45*). Caernarfon has a rich history, as you'll find out at the **Segontium Roman Fort and Museum** (tel: 01286 675625; www. nationaltrust.org.uk; daily 10am–4pm; free), which sits to the southeast of the town centre on the A4085, where the foundations of a fort garrisoned by the 20th Augustan legion can still be seen. The Romans had built the fort here to control the coast around Anglesey, which was where the Druids made their last stand against the invaders. The site was of great strategic importance as it also helped to protect against attacks from across the Irish Sea. Occupied from around AD 77 to AD 394, Segontium garrisoned around 1,000 soldiers and was also an important administrative centre in Wales. The museum contains Roman artefacts and tells the story of the occupation of Wales.

Caernarfon Castle
But above all Caernarfon is synonymous with the magnificent **Castle**

Left: fishing boats in Caernarfon Bay. **Above**: Caernarfon Castle, part of Edward I's network of fortifications throughout Wales.

(tel: 01286 677617; www.cadw.wales. gov.uk; Nov–Feb Mon–Sat 10am–4pm, Sun 11am–4pm; Mar–June and Sept–Oct daily 9.30am–5pm; July–Aug daily 9.30am–6pm). This enormous castle was built by Edward I and joined part of his network of fortifications in Wales; the intention was to create a royal residence and seat of administrative power. It overlooks the Menai Strait and was of great symbolic significance: it and the new surrounding town effectively erasing all visible signs of Welshness and embodying Edward I's imperial dreams. Having ended the power of the native Welsh princes, the king even ensured that his son (later Edward II) was born at Caernarfon, and then conferred on him the title of Prince of Wales.

Although begun, along with Conwy Castle, in 1283, it was to be 43 years before the building was complete. Twice unsuccessfully besieged by Owain Glyndwr, fought over during the Civil Wars and captured by Par-

Above: the grassy interior of Caernarfon Castle.

liamentary forces in 1646, the castle was finally condemned for demolition in 1660. Happily the exterior walls and three towers remain intact and are hugely impressive, though most of the interior has been lawned. The

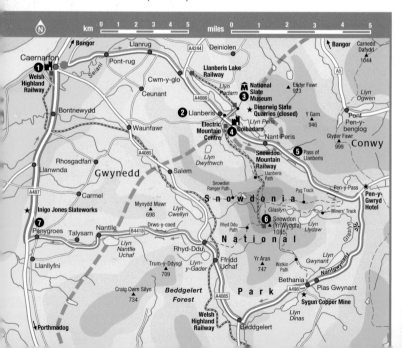

present Prince of Wales was invested here on 1 July 1969, an event which caused some local controversy which was perhaps not surprising given the castle's history. Queen's Tower houses the fascinating **Regimental Museum** (tel: 01286 673362; www.rwf museum.org.uk; Sept–Oct and Mar–June daily 9.30am–5pm; July–Aug 9.30am–6pm; Nov–end Feb Mon–Sat 10am–4pm, Sun 11am–4pm; free) of the Royal Welch Fusiliers (they still use the ancient spelling of their name). The oldest regiment in Wales, their mascot is a goat.

Much of the town's present countenance dates from the 19th century, when it became the location of a thriving slate port. Victoria Dock is home to **Galeri Caernarfon** (tel: 01286 685252; www.galericaernar fon.com) a striking arts venue, whose stylish exterior reflects the area's industrial heritage. It has a 400-seat theatre, a cinema and a gallery, as well as a café.

North of Caernarfon, at Plas Menai, lies the **National Outdoor Centre** (tel: 01248 670964; www. plasmenai.co.uk), which offers a host of aqua-based activities, from kayaking to windsurfing and powerboating.

LLANBERIS

From Caernarfon, take the A4086 east to the shores of Llyn Padarn and **Llanberis ❷**. The town's location at the foot of Snowdon and its plethora of visitor attractions ensure a brisk peak season trade, though during the winter a rather more traditional Welsh character is revealed. To the left of the A4086,

Below: looking down on Caernarfon from the vantage point of the castle.

Ⓕ Castles in Wales

William the Conqueror was the first to build castles in Wales, using them to impose his authority on the area. Most Norman castles are in the south and along the English/Welsh border. In the 13th century, Welsh princes began to build their own castles, which were smaller than Norman structures and were sited on craggy outcrops – such as Dolwyddelan. The final wave of castle building was carried out by Edward I and was concentrated in North Wales, the idea being to create a defensive ring that would subdue the country for good.

Above: Caernarfon Castle was meant to symbolise English dominance.

on the south shore of Llyn Padarn, is the **Electric Mountain Centre** (tel: 01286 870636; www.fhc. co.uk/electric_mountain.htm; daily 9.30am–5.30pm; booking advised), the base for bus tours leading for half a mile (0.8km) into the bowels of the Dinorwig Pumped Storage Power Station, the largest underground power station in Europe, commissioned in 1984. Visitors are shown the turbines and generators, and there is an underground film show.

Near the eastern end of Llanberis is the **Snowdon Mountain Railway** (tel: 0844 493 8120; www.snowdon railway.co.uk; late Mar–early Nov daily, subject to weather and demand). Whether ridden in or simply watched, the little trains make a stirring sight as they leave Llanberis station and work their way up the mountain. The rack-and-pinion track was laid in an astonishing 72 days during 1895–6, using Swiss techniques, and is the only public railway of its type in the UK. Since then increasing numbers of visitors have enjoyed the excursion – an hour each way with 30 minutes at the summit. The line runs for just over 4 miles (6km). The **Llanberis Track** up Snowdon, roughly parallel to the railway, begins from the road oppo-

site the Royal Victoria Hotel. It is the most popular path to the summit.

LLANBERIS LAKE RAILWAY

The A4086 next approaches Llyn Peris and the remains of the vast hillside terraces of Dinorwig Slate Quarries, which closed in 1969. Covering 700 acres (280 hectares) and rising some 2,000ft (600m) up the flanks of Elidir Fawr, they were the largest of their kind in Britain during their heyday, employing over 3,000 men. The slate was taken to Port Dinorwig (Y Felinheli) on the Menai Strait by narrow-gauge railway, now partially revived as the

Above: traversing the mountain on Snowdon Mountain Railway. **Below**: an easier way to reach the summit.

passenger-carrying **Llanberis Lake Railway** (tel: 01286 870549; www. lake-railway.co.uk; Apr–Aug daily, check timetable for other dates). Trains leave from Gilfach Ddu station and run along the lakeside. The line is set in Padarn Country Park, an 800-acre (320-hectare) area which has numerous walking trails and boating on the lake.

Beneath the slate quarries, in the original Dinorwig Quarry buildings, is the **National Slate Museum** ❸ (tel: 029 2057 3700; www.museum wales.ac.uk; Easter–Oct daily 10am–5pm, Nov–Easter Sun–Fri 10am–4pm; free), where visitors can still see craftsmen cutting slate 'the old way' and are shown the gigantic water-wheel, the biggest in mainland Britain and, with a diameter of 54ft (17m), one of the biggest in the world. You can also explore former quarrymen's cottages, moved here from nearby Tanygrisiau, and see a 3D presentation on the story of slate. By the museum is the **Snowdonia Rope Centre** (tel: 01286 872310; www.ropes andladders.co.uk; daily 9am–5pm but can vary with demand, booking recommended), a high-level outdoor climbing centre aimed at families. The aerial challenge course has bridges, swings and a zip line.

The adjacent **Dolbadarn Castle** ❹ (tel: 01443 336000; www.cadw. wales.gov.uk; daily 10am–4pm), built on a grassy knoll to guard the overland route between Caernarfon and Conwy, is today a ruin presiding over a tract of Welsh landscape ravaged and re shaped by civilisation: changed indeed from 1800 when the artist J.M.W. Turner sketched and painted the 50ft (15m) round tower silhouetted against a lowering sky. The fortress, built in the 13th century by Llewellyn the Great, holds a grim history. Owain ap Grufydd was imprisoned here for 22 years

Above: the round tower of Dolbadarn castle, near Llanberis.

❻ Safety on Snowdon

Before setting off on any of the ascents of Snowdon, make sure you're well prepared with good walking boots, waterproofs, warm layers, map, a compass, a whistle (to attract attention in emergencies), food and water. Let someone know the route you're taking and check the weather forecast. No matter how lovely and sunny it may be at the bottom, conditions can change rapidly on the mountain.

Above: properly attired walkers on the summit of Snowdon.

Above: the rugged Pass of Llanberis, created by two lakes cutting through the mountain pass, is well known amongst rock climbers.

by his brother Llewellyn the Last when they were fighting for control of North Wales. Another of Llewellyn the Last's brothers, Dafydd, made Dolbadarn a base for resistance against Edward I's incursions into Wales, but the castle was seized in 1282 and Dafydd captured and executed in 1283.

PASS OF LLANBERIS

Grey crags soar above skirts of scree and boulders close in beyond Nant Peris. With innumerable classic routes on the precipices of Glyder Fawr to the north and Snowdon to the south, the **Pass of Llanberis** ❺ has become a mecca for rock climbers. Halfway up the pass on the left soars the great prow of Dinas Cromlech. Breakthroughs in the evolution of climbing took place here with Joe Brown's ascent of Cenotaph Corner in the 1950s, Pete Livesey's Right Wall and Ron Fawcett's Fly on the Wall in the 1970s. One of the most famous routes by Joe Brown and Don Whillans was Cemetery Gates. The road (built *c.*1830) is narrow and what few parking bays exist are usually occupied

by climbers' vehicles. It is impossible not to be moved by the awesome scenery, even from a car, and many visitors are naturally tempted to park at **Pen-y-Pass**, 1,168ft (356m). However, the car park there is notoriously over-subscribed (and expensive) so an alternative is to catch the bus up and back from Llanberis. The inn at the pass, where George Mallory once stayed, is now a YHA hostel.

TRACKS TO SNOWDON

There are six major paths to the summit of **Snowdon** ❻ (Yr Wyddfa in Welsh). The Llanberis Path starts back in Llanberis, while starting points for the remainder will be found on this stretch of the route. Behind the car park at Pen-y-Pass begin two popular paths to Snowdon's peak (3,560ft (1,085m). The **Miners' Track**, the easier of the two, was constructed in 1856 to serve the Britannia Copper Mine situated high under the mountain's east face. The **Pig Track** or 'Pyg Track' (after Bwlch y Moch – Pass of the Pigs – which it crosses) is more rugged and much more challenging. Both tracks converge higher up, ascending the zig zags to join the Llanberis Path and railway for the final 300ft (90m) to the summit. The Miners' Track, as far as Llyn Llydaw, presents no difficulties and makes an enjoyable ramble. Both routes take about 6 hours to complete.

Cut into the steep face of Moel Berfedd and with dizzy views down Nantgwynant, the road descends to the Pen y Gwryd Hotel. Pen y Gwryd translates as 'Head of Cai's Fathom-wide Pass', from Cai, one of Arthur's knights who, legend has it, was massive enough to block the pass with his outstretched hands. The old inn here continues to accommodate hillgoers as well as passing tourists in a style appropriate to its unique situation and history. Not only did it once host the pioneers of early British rock climbing but Everest expeditions based their

training programmes here.

Turn right at the T-junction and follow the A498 towards Beddgelert. Between Llyn Gwynant and Llyn Dinas, a small car park at **Pont Bethania** denotes the start of Snowdon's **Watkin Path**. Constructed by Sir Edward Watkin, a railway engineer and early protagonist of the Channel Tunnel, it

Below: the view indicator (toposcope) on Snowdon's summit.

Ⓥ Hafod Eryri

The visitor centre on the summit of Snowdon, which officially opened in 2009, was built to replace Sir Clough Williams-Ellis' 1935 structure. Constructed in granite, in contemporary style, with expansive views from its huge glass frontage, the centre has to withstand the uncompromising weather conditions on the summit – wind speeds can reach 150mph (240kph). It offers refreshments and information on the mountain, as well as serving as the terminus for the Snowdon Mountain Railway.

Above: Hafod Eryri, the highest building in Wales and England.

THE PASS OF ABERGLASLYN
By NORMAN WILKINSON R.R.I.

NORTH WALES
FOR HOLIDAYS

was officially opened at a ceremony in 1892 by the great statesman, W.E. Gladstone. As the commemorative plaque further up the path records: 'The Multitude sang Cymric hymns and Land of my Fathers'.

Ⓢ Shop for Slate

At the Inigo Jones Slateworks you can purchase all sorts of items made of fine Welsh slate, such as nameplates, plaques and even jewellery. You can pick up bags of slate chippings for the garden, and even have items made to order, such as kitchen worktops and windowsills.

Above: slate souvenirs, some displaying the Welsh dragon.

Left: 1930s poster advertising the Beddgelert area. **Right**: turning slate on a lathe, Inigo Jones Slateworks.

BEDDGELERT FOREST PARK

From Beddgelert *(see Tour 3, p.42)* continue on the A4085 Caernarfon road. Foothills to the west are clothed in the pine and larch of **Beddgelert Forest Park**. Camping in the Forest has a large and well-appointed campsite (0845 130 8224) here, as well as a number of waymarked trails. Further on lies Llyn-y-Gader, an anglers' lake mirroring the peaks along the Nantlle Ridge at its back. A little south of **Rhyd-Ddu Village** will be found a car park for Snowdon's **Rhyd-Ddu Path**, one of the easier paths to the summit of Snowdon. In clear visibility almost the whole route to the peak can be seen from here.

Less than 2 miles (3km) further along the A4085 stands the Snowdon Ranger youth hostel set above the waters of Llyn Cwellyn, home to the rare char, or red-bellied Alpine trout. It was here, on his journey through Wales in 1854, that George Borrow chatted with a local guide who offered to lead him up Snowdon and whose profession gave the **Snowdon Ranger Path**, another of the official paths to the summit, its name.

PENYGROES

Instead of driving straight back to Caernarfon, you now take a less direct but more rewarding route. Turn west at Rhyd-ddu onto the B4418. Quite soon the road passes Llyn Dywarchen and squeezes through Drws-y-coed (The Wooded Pass) between the crags and scree of Craig y Bera and the menacing northern precipice of Y Garn to reach the Nantlle Valley (Dyffryn Nantlle). Passing Llyn Nantlle Uchaf, the Talysarn slate quarries and

terraces of miners' cottages, you soon reach **Penygroes** ❼, with its trim chapels and memories of altogether busier times over a century ago.

INIGO JONES SLATEWORKS

To conclude the tour turn right along the A487, back towards Caernarfon.

About a mile (1.6km) to the north, between Penygroes and Llanwnda, is the **Inigo Jones Slateworks** (tel: 01286 830242; www.inigojones.co.uk; daily 9am–5pm), which dates back to 1861. Here visitors can go on self-guided tours of the workshops and browse in the showroom for a variety of slate souvenirs.

Ⓔ Eating Out

Caernarfon
Black Boy Inn
Northgate St; tel: 01286 673604; www.black-boy-inn.com; Mon–Thur noon–9pm, Fri–Sun until 9.30pm.
This 16th-century inn is a popular place with both locals and visitors. It's a good place to try some traditional dishes such as lobscouse, a stew of black beef with onions and vegetables. The menu may also feature pub favourites like steak and ale pie, and a large Yorkshire pudding filled with sausage and vegetables. ££
Castell
33 Y Maes; tel: 01286 678895; daily noon–9.30pm.
Lots of fresh Welsh produce on the menu at this restaurant in the centre of Caernarfon – they cure their own ham and all desserts are home-made.

Fish features prominently – hake served with chips, or Menai mussels, and there are vegetarian choices such as pea and parmesan tart. Among the desserts you might find lemon posset, or a fresh rhubarb crumble. ££

Llanberis
The Peak
86 High Street; tel: 01286 872777; www.peakrestaurant.co.uk; Wed–Sat from 7pm.
This welcoming restaurant serves a varied menu featuring Eastern and Western dishes. You might find Thai fish cakes for starters, and mains like Welsh lamb shank or rib eye steak. There are vegetarian options too. Desserts might include summer pudding or a chocolate tart. ££

Welsh Language

Don't be surprised if you go into a shop in North Wales and find that you're unable to understand what people are saying – the ancient Celtic language of Welsh is still widely spoken here

Beneath its veneer of tourism, Snowdonia is a stronghold of Welsh culture and tradition where one of Europe's oldest languages may be heard in everyday use. Welsh is the native tongue of a large proportion of the population – particularly around Caernarfon; and most people can speak and understand the language.

Welsh belongs to the Celtic family of languages and, as one of the Brythonic Celtic tongues, is closely related to Cornish and Breton. Its origins stem from the Celtic Iron Age people who moved into Wales from the continent between about 550 BC and AD 50. Although the language was almost certainly being spoken as early as the 6th century AD, some of the first examples of written Welsh occur in tales from the Mabinogion, a collection of mythical stories written down around the 13th century, but of much earlier origin *(see p.38)*.

ROMAN INFLUENCE

During the Roman occupation, the language of the rulers had an influence on the Welsh tongue, as can be seen with words such as caws (cheese), pont (bridge) and ffenestre (window). Welsh,

Welsh Words and Phrases

Some useful phrases:

- **Bore da** – Good morning
- **Nos da** – Good night
- **Hwyl fawr** – Good bye
- **Diolch** – Thank you
- **Dim diolch** – No thank you
- **Faint?** – How much?
- **Os gwelwch chi'n dda** – please
- **Gwely a brecwast** – bed and breakfast

Some Welsh words:

- **Afon** – river
- **Bara** – bread
- **Bryn** – hill
- **Bws** – bus
- **Croeso** – welcome
- **Cymraeg** – Welsh
- **Cymru** – Wales
- **Eglwys** – church
- **Gwesty** – hotel
- **Mynydd** – mountain
- **Tafarn** – pub
- **Ysbyty** – hospital

however, still thrived until the 16th-century Acts of Union ruled that English should be the only language of the courts. However, the language still survived, partly thanks to William Morgan, who translated the Bible into Welsh.

It was in the 19th century that the language fell into decline, thanks to an educational report of 1847. Written by English commissioners, it stressed the importance of the use of English,

Main Picture: a sign for Llanfair PG's full name, the longest place name in Britain.
Top Left and Left: Welsh and English co-exist on a Wrexham signpost and a National Park plaque.

rather than Welsh, in schools. Children were forbidden to speak the language, a stick called a 'Welsh not' being used as a form of punishment if they did so. Welsh could easily have gone the way of Cornish, and became almost a forgotten language. However, pressure groups fought to keep it alive, and, in the 21st century, devolution has ensured that Wales is now, officially at least, a bilingual country. Much of the country's commerce and administration is undertaken in Welsh, schools and road signs are bilingual and there are Welsh TV and radio channels. The National Assembly, in Cardiff, treats both English and Welsh equally.

Tour 5

The Lleyn Peninsula

Running for 75 miles (121km) around the Lleyn Peninsula, this full day's tour takes you on a circuit of one of the quietest corners of North Wales; an area rich in history

It is hard to look at a map of the Lleyn Peninsula and not be reminded of Cornwall. The western Lleyn (pronounced 'thlinn') has even been dubbed the 'Land's End of North Wales'. But over the centuries it has suffered none of Cornwall's intensive exploitation for mineral ores and china clay. Neither has it sustained so many pressures in more recent times from the holiday industry. A scattering of modest resorts the Lleyn may have, but elsewhere the landscape is hilly and agricultural. You sense, in the walled pastures and isolated farmsteads, a foreignness reminiscent of Brittany, perhaps, or southwest Ireland. It is indisputably Celtic.

The Lleyn's roads were not built for motor traffic. Narrow and twist-ing, they meander between high banks and tall hedges with occasional sudden views of a shapely hillside or the glint of sunshine on waves. It's a great place to explore on foot or on a bicycle.

Highlights

- Criccieth
- Lloyd George Museum
- Pwllheli
- Plas Glyn-y-Weddw
- Abersoch
- Bardsey Island
- Porth Dinllaen
- Llanaelhaearn
- St Beuno's Church

The coastline, which covers nearly 100 miles (161km) is a mostly unspoilt Area of Outstanding Natural Beauty, alternating between savage cliffs and golden sands whose inaccessibility guarantees seclusion.

CRICCIETH

This route starts at **Criccieth ❶**, a holiday playground in Victorian times. The town's central green imparts an intimate village flavour to this essen-

Left: a fishing boat being towed towards the sea at Abersoch.
Below: Criccieth's town and 13th-century castle on its headland.

tially family resort. Almost dividing the town in half, **Criccieth Castle** (tel: 01766 522227; www.cadw.wales. gov.uk; Apr–end Oct daily 10am–5pm, Nov–Mar Fri–Sat 9.30am–4pm, Sun 11am–4pm) perches on a grassy headland between a pebble strand backed by hotel terraces on Marine Drive and, to the east, a great arc of safe bathing beach and promenade. Visit the castle ruin if you can, both for its chequered history and for the magnificent views. Built by the Welsh in the 13th century, contemporary with Llewellyn the Great, it was taken by Edward I who extended and refortified it, and incorporated it into his

Above: a view from Abersoch on the Lleyn peninsula. Abersoch is ideal for water-sports and horse-riding.

'Iron Ring' of coastal fortifications in 1283. Owain Glyndwr's Welsh uprising besieged and sacked the castle 140 years later, leaving it much as we find it today.

LLANYSTUMDWY

Take the A497 coast road past **Llanystumdwy** to visit its **Lloyd George Museum** ❷ (tel: 01766 522071; www.gwynedd.gov.uk; May Mon–Fri 10.30am–5pm, June Mon–Sat 10.30am–5pm, July–Sept daily 10.30am–5pm, Oct Mon–Fri 11am–4pm), entirely devoted

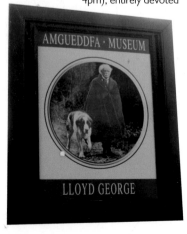

to the life and times of this great Liberal politician, who was Prime Minister from 1916–22. Born in Manchester, of Welsh parents, he came to the village after his father died when he was a small child, and lived with his mother in Highgate Cottage opposite the Feathers Inn until 1880. His uncle's shoemaking workshop next door has been imaginatively re-created. Winston Churchill said of Lloyd George: 'He was the greatest Welshman which that unconquerable race has produced since the age of the Tudors'. Memorabilia on display ranges from political cartoons to the pencil with which he wrote his memoirs, and there's a film about his life. Now continue along the coast to Pwllheli.

PWLLHELI

Pwllheli ❸ is the largest of the Lleyn's settlements and a market town since 1355. It was once a busy port, though it declined after the construction of Porthmadog. The newish marina here can berth 400 boats. Pwllheli is probably best known as the place where the Welsh National Party, Plaid Cymru, was founded in 1925. There are two beaches here: Glan y Don beach (also known as Aberech), a

collection of paintings displayed in the fine rooms. There's also a permanent collection of fine Swansea and Nantgarw porcelain and a shop where you can purchase arts and crafts.

ABERSOCH

Follow the coast road to **Abersoch** ❺, set in a bay called St Tudwal's Road. This and the two uninhabited offshore islands take their name from a 6th-century Brittany saint who fled from religious persecution in the Dark Ages and founded a monastic cell on St Tudwal's Island East. Ruins of an 800-year-old chapel there can be seen from boat trips around the islands (tel: 01758 712646; weather permitting, in season). In Abersoch itself will be found the Lleyn Peninsula's only dyed-in-the-wool holiday resort.

lovely sandy stretch to the east, and South Beach, stretching for around 3 miles (5km) to the west. They offer great bathing. Pwllheli is the northern terminus of the scenic **Cambrian Coast Railway** (www.thecambrian line.co.uk), which extends down to Aberystwyth.

LLANBEDROG

Now continue following the coast, to reach **Llanbedrog**, home to **Plas Glyn-y-Weddw** ❹ (tel: 01758 740763; www.oriel.org.uk; daily 10am–5pm). This Victorian Gothic mansion was purpose-built in the 19th century to house an art collection, and is today a striking art gallery with a changing

Ⓥ Panoramas on the Lleyn

There are some wonderful viewpoints on the Lleyn. The top of Criccieth Castle is an excellent vantage point on a fine day, while Plas Glyn-y-Weddw, the Victorian mansion at Llanbedrog, offers sea views that seem to stretch forever. Then there's Plas yn Rhiw, near Abersoch, where you can look right across to Cardigan Bay.

Above: the art gallery in Plas Glyn-y-Weddw is reputedly haunted.

Above: the Lleyn peninsula runs from Caernarfon to Porthmadog.

Above: the picturesque beach huts at Abersoch can be rented. Abersoch's main beach is sheltered and the sea is used by both swimmers and water-sports fans.

A lively harbour, fine beach, narrow shop-lined streets, restaurants, pubs and hotels, as well as extensive complexes of caravans and chalets, all betray a wide appeal.

LLANENGAN TO RHIW

Head southwest on the unclassified road over to the southern end of Porth Neigwl (Hell's Mouth), above which stands the little village of **Llanengan**. The unrestored, twin-naved **Parish Church** dates from the 15th century, with roots almost a thousand years earlier. Its bells and sacred vessels were brought over from St Mary's Abbey on Bardsey Island whose pilgrims would have called at Llanengan on their journey west.

Taking the northbound by road across the Afon Soch leads to pretty Llangian hamlet. The churchyard contains a 5th- or 6th-century Roman stone bearing an inscription in Latin which declares that the remains of 'Melus the Doctor, son of Martinus, lie here'. In the whole of Britain there is no other record of an early Christian burial mentioning the deceased's profession.

Bear left and left again to the northern end of Hell's Mouth, its anglicised name testimony to the threat this vast crescent bay once posed to sailing ships which risked being driven ashore in southwesterly gales. Ahead there is a steep climb to **Rhiw** ❻, highest village on the Lleyn, where stands a delightful 16th-century Welsh manor house surrounded by its own grounds and ornamental garden. **Plas yn Rhiw** is owned by the National Trust (tel: 01758 780219; www.nationaltrust. org.uk; late-Mar–May and Sept Thur–Sun noon–5pm, June–July Wed–Mon noon–5pm, Aug daily noon–5pm, Oct Thur–Sun noon–4pm). It was almost derelict when it was purchased in the 1930s by the Keating sisters, friends of the Welsh poet R.S. Thomas who lived in a cottage on the estate.

ABERDARON

Three miles (5km) farther west the attractive little fishing village of **Aberdaron** ❼ nestles in a fold at the back of its cliff-girt bay, sheltered from all winds but the south. In good weather there are boat trips to view Bardsey Island. The final resting place

Above Left: Llangian hamlet can be visited on the way from Llanengan to Rhiw.
Above Right: locally caught crab for sale in Aberdaron.

for 14th-century pilgrims en route for Bardsey was Aberdaron's Y-Gegin-Fawr (The Big Kitchen) near the old hump-backed bridge; it is now a café-cum-gift shop. The Henfaes Centre next to the bridge has information on things to see and do in the area. Recently constructed sea defences reveal Aberdaron's vulnerability to marine erosion. Note how the Norman doorway of **St Hywyn's Church** has been weathered by centuries of storms. When built some 500 years ago, it was set back at a safe distance from the shore, but now its cemetery rises incongruously from the beach and the building only survives thanks to the provision of its own sea wall.

BARDSEY ISLAND

Tentacle-like, single-track lanes reach out towards 'land's end'. For a path to the shore, go via Uwchmynydd to the end of the public road beneath the rocky fist of Mynydd Mawr. Alternatively, drive on up the concrete track to old coastguard buildings on the 524ft (160m) summit. All around the tip of the Lleyn are uninterrupted views to **Bardsey Island** (or 'Ynys

Enlli', 'island of the currents' in Welsh). Founded in the 6th century, the Abbey of St Mair (St Mary) was a place of pilgrimage for hundreds of years: it was said that three pilgrimages to Bardsey were equivalent to one pilgrimage to Rome. Many holy men stayed on and were buried there, giving rise to the title 'Island of 20,000 Saints'. The abbey ruins lie beneath 548ft (167m) Mynydd Enlli, roughly in line with the lighthouse. During the early 20th century, Bardsey was still inhabited by a fishing and farming community, but today it is largely a seabird sanctuary, visited by

F Boat Trips to Bardsey

Various operators offer boat trips to Bardsey Island. You can take a one-hour cruise around the island from Pwllheli with Shearwater (tel: 01758 612251) or a three-hour trip, in which you land on the island, with Enlli Charter (tel: 0845 811 3655), who operate from Pwllheli and Aberdaron. Bardsey Boat Trips also run day trips from Aberdaron (tel: 07971 769895).

Above: the coastal fishing village Morfa Nefyn. Park here to stretch your legs on the walk to Porth Dinllaen.

occasional boatloads of ornithologists bound for the observatory. Cardigan Bay down to St David's Head, the Snowdonia peaks and even, appropriately for their shared Celtic heritage, the Wicklow Mountains of Ireland, can be seen from high ground.

PORTH DINLLAEN

Return to Aberdaron and follow the B4413 northeast to Pen-y-groeslon. Here turn left on the B4417 to Tudweiliog. Continue along the B4417 to **Morfa Nefyn**, where there's a National Trust car park. It's best to park here and walk the mile (1.6km) or so of track to the hamlet of **Porth Dinllaen** ❽, acquired by the National Trust in 1994. The picturesque sandy cove backed by neat cottages and a water-

Above: learn Welsh as a second language in Nant Gwrtheryn.

front pub had once been earmarked as the packet port for Ireland. In 1806 William Madocks, Member of Parliament for Boston, Lincolnshire, formed a company to build a harbour at Porth Dinllaen, but two years later when the necessary Parliamentary Bill was introduced it failed to gain support and Holyhead was selected instead. Madocks' ambition resurfaced in 1844 when Porth Dinllaen established its own railway company. However, the Chester and Holyhead line, already built, proved the decisive factor in the final abandonment of Madocks' scheme and Porth Dinllaen sank into quiet obscurity. Only Madocks' straight road to Pwllheli, designed for speeding transit of the Irish mail, and his development of Porthmadog and Tremadog as staging posts on the route to London (see *Tour 3, p.44*) remain.

NANT GWRTHERYN

Continue on the B4417 through Nefyn to Llithfaen. A mile (1.6km) to the north at Nant Gwrtheryn is the **Welsh Language Centre** (www.nantgwrtheyrn.org), housed in a once-derelict quarry village, even today a wild and remote spot. There's a visitor centre and a café. **Llanaelhaearn** ❾ is a small village at the foot of Lleyn's three most distinctive peaks known as

Yr Eifl (The Forks), or by their English name The Rivals. The highest, central top reaches 1,850ft (564m), the lowest, to seaward, 1,457ft (444m). But it is the eastern peak that holds the greatest interest, for its summit is crowned by the remains of Tre'r Ceiri (Town of the Giants). This ancient fortified settlement, probably of Bronze Age origin and containing well-preserved hut circles, can be reached by a footpath off the B4417 less than a mile (1.6km) southwest of Llanaelhaearn.

ST BEUNO'S CHURCH

Bear north along the coast on the A499, to reach **Clynnog-fawr** to visit the surprisingly large 15th-century church of **St Beuno** ❿, which stands on the site of a 7th-century monastery. Inside is a medieval wooden chest, a reminder that the church was once an important stopping point on the pilgrim route to Bardsey Island.

Now turn south on the A499, follow it for a while then turn left onto the B4354 through Chwilog, to visit **Penarth Fawr** (tel: 01443 336000; www.cadw.wales.gov.uk; daily 10am–5pm) a 15th-century hall house that belonged to a wealthy family. It's noted for its fine timber roof. This stretch of road was part of Madocks' proposed London to Porth Dinllaen turnpike which he claimed would have been 30 miles (48km) shorter than the route to Holyhead. You now return to Criccieth.

E Eating Out

Pwllheli
Plas Bodegroes
Tel: 01758 612363; www.bodegroes.co.uk; Tue–Sat dinner, Sun lunch; booking required.
This Michelin-starred restaurant with rooms is in a charming Georgian country house, with pretty gardens. The dining room is elegant, with local art on the walls. Welsh produce features on the modern British menu, which might include dishes such as local sea bass with crab, ginger and pak choi and a *bara brith* bread-and-butter pudding for dessert. £££
Y Bryncynan
Morfa Nefyn, nr Pwllheli; tel: 01758 720879; www.bryncynan.com; daily noon–9.30pm.
A family-friendly inn with an extensive menu ranging from steaks to burgers. There are pub favourites like cottage pie and steak and ale pie, as well as ploughmans' and sandwiches. ££

Criccieth
Caffi Cwrt
Y Maes; daily.
This traditional tea shop in the heart of Criccieth is set in an atmospheric old building with wooden beams. It offers hot drinks, scones and cakes. £
Llanbedrog
Tremfan Hall; tel: 01758 740169; www.tremfanhall.com; daily from 6.30pm in peak season (approx July–Sept), otherwise Wed–Sun from 6.30pm; also open Sun lunch.
Lovely country house overlooking Tremadog Bay, offering a varied menu of modern British dishes. Choices might include starters of Menai oysters or Llyn crab pot, followed by Moroccan lamb tagine or roast skate wing. For dessert you might find *crème brûlée* or pecan pie. £££
Poachers Restaurant
66–68 High Street; tel: 01766 522512; www.poachersrestaurant.co.uk; Mon–Sat from 6pm.
This contemporary restaurant serves dishes such as Welsh black beef lasagne and Welsh pork loin steak. For dessert try their apple, walnut and caramel cake. The menu changes with the seasons and there are vegetarian choices available. ££

Tour 6

Tremadog Bay to the Mawddach Estuary

This 53-mile (85km) one-day circuit takes you to the fantasy town of Portmeirion and picturesque Harlech Castle, along the coast to Barmouth and then inland

On this route you reach the southern parts of Snowdonia National Park. Ardudwy, the high and ancient upland region between the Vale of Ffestiniog and the Mawddach estuary, guards its secrets well. Many of the Mabinogion's heroic sagas are based here. Ireland, just across the sea, seems to have a presence, visible in the primeval stones named *cyttiau wyddelod* – Irishman's huts. Modern roads only tickle the foothills and it is rough country to walk in. In his book *On Foot in North Wales*, published in 1933, Patrick Monkhouse writes about an ascent of Rhinog Fawr: 'it exacts more perspiration to the yard than any other mile in Wales…'. This is where experienced

local walkers come when they want to escape the crowds. Fortunately the coastline is a softer place with dunes and sandy beaches extending all the way to Barmouth, a classic holiday resort. Watching over the seas is Harlech Castle, which juts defiantly skyward.

Left and Right: views around Italianate village Portmeirion, including the Pantheon and Bell Tower.

PORTMEIRION

Your route starts in Porthmadog, terminus for the vintage Ffestiniog Railway (see *Tour 3, p.45*). Shortly after crossing The Cob, take the driveway on the right to **Portmeirion** ❶ (tel: 01766 770000; www.portmeirion-village. com; daily 9.30am–7.30pm), a folly par excellence which draws in visitors from across the globe. Following a tour of Italy when he became captivated by the fishing village of Portofino, the architect Clough Williams-Ellis searched for a suitable site on which to create an Italianate fantasy of his own. In 1925, quite by chance, he was offered the present land, then derelict, beside the Dwyryd Estuary not far from his ancestral home. Work began in 1926, with the village developing around an Italian-style piazza, and dotted with arches, statues and fountains. His declared mission was to 'show that one could develop even a very beautiful place without defiling it and, given sufficient care, you could even enhance what was given as a backdrop'. Williams-Ellis always intended Portmeirion to awaken visitors' interest in architecture, decor and landscaping. In amongst the extravaganza of small-scale, pastel-coloured Mediterranean buildings, including shops and restaurants, appear architectural oddments from all over Britain, some rescued from demolition sites by Williams-Ellis himself.

The 19th-century house standing on the original site became the Portmeirion Hotel which hosted many celebrities during the 1930s. Bernard Shaw stayed there, as did the playwright Noël Coward, who wrote *Blithe Spirit* here. Castell Deudraeth, a Victorian mansion on the estate, was built for

a local MP. Williams-Ellis purchased it and used it as a hotel for a while in the 1930s. It has now been restored and is a hotel again.

Portmeirion was the main location for cult 1960s TV series, *The Prisoner*, and still attracts many fans. There are walks above the sandy shoreline backed by 70 acres (28 hectares) of subtropical gardens as well as through woodland to little bays on the peninsula's south side. (NB: Strong tidal currents make bathing dangerous.) On a fine day it would be easy to spend a whole day here.

LLANDECWYN CHURCH

Return to the A487 and fork right opposite Penrhyndeudraeth's church to pass the railway station on the scenic Cambrian Coast Line between Pwllheli and Aberystwyth (see *Tour 5, p.65*). In fact, the road curves across the Afon Dwyryd beside the railway line on a toll bridge to Llandecwyn station before heading for the lake-dotted foothills north of the main Rhinog range, en-

Above: Llandecwyn Church sits between the two tranquil Tecwyn lakes, known for their trout fishing.

countered more closely later. Rather than following the A496 south, stay on this byroad via Bryn Bwbach. Up to the left, halfway between the two Tecwyn lakes, stands the isolated little **Llandecwyn Church**, which has medieval origins and is also a magnificent viewpoint. Resuming your southerly progress, fork right after a couple of miles at Eisingrug, to reach the B4573.

Alternatively, for superb panoramas over Tremadog Bay, stay on the narrow mountain road climbing the shoulder of Moel Goedog, 1,211ft (369m), an area rich in prehistoric remains. Either way, the next port of call will be Harlech.

HARLECH

At one time **Harlech ❷** was a fashionable coastal resort, attracting famous people such as the composer Gustav Holst, the poet Robert Graves, Sir Henry Wood (of the Proms) and George Bernard Shaw. It's even said that nude bathing began here in the 1930s. The town is small, so easy to explore, and very attractive with winding streets. It makes a good base for walks and drives in this part of Snowdonia – and golfers will love its 18 hole, par 69, internationally renowned links golf course, Royal St David's.

Harlech Castle (tel: 01766 780552; www.cadw.wales.gov.uk; Nov–Feb Mon–Sat 10am–4pm, Sun 11am–4pm, June and Sept–Oct daily 9.30am–5pm, July–Aug until 6pm) entirely

Right: Harlech Castle, part of Edward I's iron ring of fortresses.

dominates the little hillside town. Designated a Unesco World Heritage Site, its square-cut profile atop a 200ft (60m) -high crag is visible from many miles distant.

Work on the castle began in 1283, after Edward I's conquest of Wales. It was part of his iron ring of castles that was built to subdue and defend the area: each castle was within a day's march of another. Around 950 men carried out the work and the castle was completed in 1283. In 1290, as a reward for his work building this and other fortifications, James of St George, Edward I's Master of Works, became Constable of Harlech in 1290. Under his direction, Harlech Castle was given four massive towers, anchoring the great curtain walls. A huge gatehouse, rather than the more usual central keep, formed the building's strongest section. The Castle's position directly above a tidal creek (the sea has since receded about half a mile/800m) permitted victualling from the sea, and supplies from Ireland were carried up the west-side steps which still exist today.

Despite its apparent impregnability, the castle fell to Owain Glyndwr in 1404, who held a parliament here in

Ⓕ Darwin's Inspiration

As a child, Charles Darwin spent many family holidays in North Wales, and became a keen collector of the shells, fossils and insects that he found there. It sparked a lifelong interest in natural history. While a student at Cambridge, he travelled to North Wales and visited Barmouth, collecting beetles and studying its geology. The skills and knowledge he acquired were to serve him well when he took up his place on the voyage of the *Beagle*.

Above: Darwin studied the geology of Capel Curig and Caernarfon.

Left: imposing entrance to Harlech Castle. **Right**: sweeping view of Morfa Harlech, whose sand dunes, mudflats and salt marsh are protected.

1405. It was recaptured by the English within five years, but then played a starring role in the Wars of the Roses when it was held by the Lancastrians. The castle was besieged by Yorkist troops (the numbers estimated at between 7,000 and 10,000 men) and subsequently surrendered; the siege is thought to have inspired the now famous marching song *Men of Harlech*. The castle's battlements offer superb views across the sea and over to Snowdon.

MORFA HARLECH

Harlech overlooks 5 miles (8km) of dune-backed sandy beach and an expanse of reclaimed land – **Morfa Harlech** – part of which is a nature reserve. It is home to rare plants and insects that live on such soft dunes, including the Welsh mudwort, lizards and a rare species of bee. Birds such as redshank and shelduck may be spotted, while otters and water voles use nearby estuarine waterways. The reserve is west of Harlech on the A496. There's a car park, and a footpath leads to the sands.

THE RHINOGS

In complete contrast, a narrow mountain road to the east snakes uphill into Cwm Bychan where, from the road-end car park, an ascent may be made to the so-called Roman Steps. (Research suggests the paved way is more likely to have been a medieval packhorse route.) Rhinog terrain – rocks and boulders concealed beneath deep heather – is notoriously rugged. Any attempt to scale Rhinog Fawr, 2,362ft (720m), should only be made by experienced and well-equipped hillwalkers. These are, however, splendidly wild hills, a landscape of boggy hollows, bare cliffs, knobbly ridge crests and high, lonely lakes. There are only two ways cross the range: Bwlch Tyddiad with its Roman steps and Bwlch Drws Arddudwy to the south, and neither path is open to vehicular traffic. The Reverend W. Bingley, writing in the late 18th century, found the latter pass 'a place well calculated to inspire a timid mind with terror' – and certainly in poor weather it can be an intimidating place.

LLANDANWG CHURCH

South of Harlech, a right turn off the A496 at Llanfair leads to the 4th-century **Llandanwg Church** ❸. Dedicated to St Tanwg, this extraordinary church is one of the very earliest places of worship in Wales. The present building is early medieval and was used until the mid-19th century. Abandoned, it was invaded by drifting dunes, and it was not until the 1980s that it was restored. The nearby **Llanfair Slate Caverns** (tel: 01766 780247; www.llanfairslatecaverns. co.uk; Easter–Sept daily 10am–5pm,

other times vary) offer an interesting diversion and there is a Farm Park (May–Sept) that will be of interest to children. Further south on the A496 is **Llanbedr** ❹ where a tidal causeway leads out to **Shell Island**, or Mochras, an exposed, low-lying peninsula with a campsite, marina and over 200 varieties of shell deposited by unusual offshore currents. Inland, again, another narrow mountain road with picnic spots approaches the Rhinogs via Cwm Nantcol.

Never far from the railway line, the A496 proceeds south past Dyffryn Ardudwy and Tal-y-bont, nudged ever nearer the sandy shore by high ground until from Llanaber everything crowds cheek-by-jowl into the only usable corridor of land. Follow the road to reach **Barmouth** ❺.

BARMOUTH

Barmouth's Welsh name, Abermaw, a contraction of Aber-mawddach (Estuary of the Mawddach), dates

ⓚ Blue Flag Bathing

Many of the beaches in North Wales have been awarded Blue Flag status, a scheme which judges them annually for criteria such as water quality and litter management. It means that children can be assured of safe, clean bathing. Amongst those beaches with Blue Flag status are beaches at Llandudno, Criccieth, Barmouth, Prestatyn, Pwllheli and Church Bay on Anglesey.

Above: Wales currently has a record 45 beaches with Blue Flag status.

Above: view of Cadair Idris from Barmouth. Cadair Idris is one of the most popular mountains to climb in Wales, after Mount Snowdon.

back to its humble origins as a fishing port and boatyard. When the railway came in the mid-19th century, the village's extensive sandy beach and its incomparable views over the estuary to Cadair Idris quickly earned it a reputation as a holiday resort.

Four and a half acres (1.8 hectares) of cliffland above the town – **Dinas Oleu** (Fortress of Light) – represents the National Trust's very first acquisition; it was presented by Mrs F. Talbot in 1895, the year of the Trust's foundation, and a further 12 acres (4.8 hectares) were added to it in 1980. It is well signposted, and a little further east will be found the waymarked Panorama Walk providing views not only of Cadair Idris and the coast but inland over the estuary's head to the distant Aran mountains.

It is also possible to cross the railway line's timber viaduct spanning the Mawddach (always a vulnerable section of the Cambrian Coast Line and expensive to maintain) using the pedestrian walkway. Additionally a seasonal ferry runs across to the narrow-gauge Fairbourne Steam Railway on the far shore *(see Tour 9, p.103)*. Walkers and cyclists can join

the **Mawddach Trail** (www.mawddachtrail.co.uk) in Barmouth. This crosses over the estuary, then runs for 9½ miles (15km) along a disused railway line to Dolgellau.

In this region of mid-Wales the happy juxtaposition of railway stations and superb walking country opens up numerous possibilities for returning to the start of rambles by train.

TY CRWN AND TY GWYN

Just in from Barmouth Harbour (boat trips) stands **Ty Crwn**, a circular 'lock-up' built in the early 19th century to accommodate, among other offenders, drunken goldminers from the Bontddu area just upstream. There are reminders of Barmouth's maritime heritage at **Ty Gwyn**, a medieval tower house, where finds from local shipwrecks are displayed. The building is said to have been where Jaspar Tudor, Earl of Pembroke, plotted against Richard III. It was a campaign which resulted in Richard's defeat at the battle of Bosworth at the hands of Jas-

Right: boats on Mawddach estuary, which is popular with walkers, cyclists and birdwatchers.

par's nephew, Henry Tudor, who took the Crown and became Henry V I I in 1485, starting the Tudor dynasty.

In June of each year Barmouth sees the start of the **Three Peaks International Yacht Race** (www.three peaksyachtrace.co.uk) during which competitors sail to Fort William, climbing en route to the summits of Snowdon, Scafell Pike and Ben Nevis. And if the resort's present-day ambience is of 'sandcastles, donkey rides and candy floss', at least there is ample car parking and plenty of space for everyone.

MAWDDACH ESTUARY

Your route now goes inland, as the A496 bears east and traces the tree-clad northern shore of the Afon Mawddach and into former gold territory. The Welsh Gold Rush began around 1850 with the discovery of the precious yellow metal at Clogau on the western edge of the so-called Dolgellau Gold Belt which stretched in a wide arc from Bala in the east to **Bontddu ⑥** on the Mawddach estuary. After a highly profitable period between 1904 and 1906, production steadily declined and Clogau closed in 1911. The fenced-off entrance to

Ⓕ Welsh Gold

The Romans mined gold in Wales, at a site in Carmarthenshire, which was still producing gold in the 1930s. In North Wales, gold was discovered in 1854 at the Clogau mine – which had opened in 1842 to extract copper. The scarcity of this rose-coloured gold made it highly prized – and expensive – hence its use in royal jewellery.

Above: royalty has been wearing Welsh gold since the early 1920s.

the Clogau St David's gold mine can still be seen today, to the west of a lane running up from Bontddu beside the Hirgwm stream. The wedding rings of the Queen Mother (1923),

Above: the ruins of Cymer Abbey, one of the smallest and poorest Cistercian abbeys in England and Wales. Its monks farmed sheep and bred horses.

the Queen (1947), Princess Margaret (1960), Princess Anne (1973) and Diana, Princess of Wales (1981) were all crafted from the same nugget of Welsh gold found there.

CYMER ABBEY

Near Llanelltyd further east along the estuary, the New Precipice Walk skirts the slopes of Foel Ispri 1,000ft (321m) above the Afon Mawddach. The better-known Precipice Walk begins further east from car parking near Llyn Cynwch (see Tour 8, p.97). See

also the modest but evocative remains nearby of **Cymer Abbey** ❼ (daily), founded in 1198 and one of the major Cistercian foundations supported by the Princes of Gwynedd. The ruins are mainly those of the uncompleted 13th-century abbey church.

TRAWSFYNYDD AND TOMEN-Y-MUR

Across the river to the right stands Dolgellau, but you follow the A470 as it forks left at Llanelltyd and climbs back to the north, towards the starting point of the route through the Coed-y-Brenin forest. More details on this magnificent forest are given in Tour 8, but even if you're only passing it's still worth calling in at the Coed-y-Brenin Visitor Centre to the right of the main road. You can pick up details of walks and forest bicycle trails there, and there's a handy café too.

The road strikes due north to by-pass **Trawsfynydd** ❽ village, with the Rhinog mountains – the heights of Ardudwy – ranged along the western

Left: a view of the Afon Mawddach from the Precipice Walk.

skyline. From Trawsfynydd, it is possible to do a circular walk of around 3 hours to visit **Tomen-y-mur**, the site of a Roman fort built around AD 78 and occupied until AD 140. There are the remains of a bathhouse and possibly an amphitheatre. After the Romans left, it was later built on by the Normans. Details of the circular walk route are on the Snowdonia National Park website (www.eryri-npa. gov.uk). Bwlch Drws Ardudwy forms a conspicuous notch, while the highest top, Y Llethr (1,875ft/756m), lies at the southern end of the massif.

The waters of Llyn Trawsfynydd were once warmed by the reactors of the Magnox Nuclear Power Station, which is now being decommissioned.

Ignore the A470's right turn to Llan Ffestiniog and branch left at Gellilydan on a by road over to Maentwrog in the beautiful Vale of Ffestiniog (see Tour 3, p.46). Parallel to the Ffestiniog Railway which threads unseen but often heard through the forest above, the A487 heads towards Porthmadog via Penrhyndeudraeth, headquarters of the Snowdonia National Park.

Ⓔ Eating Out

Harlech
Castle Cottage
Y Llech; tel: 01766 780479; www. castlecottageharlech.co.uk; daily 7–9pm; booking essential.
This Michelin-recommended restaurant with rooms is in the centre of Harlech. The restaurant has contemporary decor, with modern Welsh art on the walls. The menu changes with the seasons, and features lots of local fish (perhaps there'll be a Barmouth lobster bisque for a starter), Welsh beef, lamb and Carmarthen ham. Desserts might include an imaginative banana and rum strudel. £££
Cemlyn
Stryd Fawr; tel: 01766 780425; www. cemlynrestaurant.com; mid-Mar–Oct Wed–Sun 10am–5pm.
This award-winning tea shop offers a wide range of loose-leaf teas, as well as delicious home-made cakes, scones and bread. It's sleek and uncluttered inside, and also has a very popular terrace which offers superb views of Harlech Castle. £

Barmouth
Bae Abermaw
Panorama Road; tel: 01341 280550; www.baeabermaw.co.uk; restaurant Tue–Sat 7–9pm, Sun lunch 12.30–

2.30pm; café daily 12.30–5pm.
This hotel restaurant serves award-winning food, with starters such as smoked haddock topped with Welsh rarebit, and mains like grilled black bream with cockles and Welsh mountain lamb. There are vegetarian choices. The café/bar serves sandwiches and afternoon teas, and there are stunning coastal views from the garden. £££
Bistro Bermo
Church Street; tel: 01341 281284; http://bistro-barmouth.co.uk; call for opening hours.
Country-style cooking and Welsh produce at this bistro. Starters might include local mussels, while typical main courses include steak and ale pie and belly of pork. ££
Ty'r Graig Castle
Llanaber Road; tel: 01341 280470; www.tyrgraigcastle.co.uk; guests Tue–Sun 6–9pm; booking advised.
Perched high above Barmouth, with great views over Cardigan Bay, is this striking Victorian building. Originally a family home, it is now an hotel with grand Victorian interiors. The restaurant serves a range of dishes such as king prawn tails, pan-fried halibut, Welsh beef, and also some vegetarian choices. ££

Tour 7

Wrexham to Bala – and back

This full day's tour of 116 miles (186km) starts in Wrexham, close to the border with England, then heads to Llangollen and on to the countryside around Bala Lake

Wrexham became prosperous in the 18th century when minerals were discovered in the surrounding countryside. It is not on the main tourist trail, but it does boast a fine church, while Llangollen, in contrast, attracts many visitors who come to enjoy the annual International Musical Eisteddfod. This corner of North Wales offers some unexpected scenic beauties, like the gloriously pastoral Ceiriog Valley. Further on, there is an unexpected wildness reminiscent of the northern Pennines of England. Villages and farmsteads cling to the edges of this 'empty quarter'. Mist often clings to its high ground, adding moisture to an already wet landscape of bog and lakes, of tumbling streams and waterfalls. Exploration on foot is not easy, but a

Highlights

- St Giles Church, Wrexham
- Erddig Hall
- Plas Newydd
- Valle Crucis Abbey
- Bala Lake
- Llyn Celyn
- The Migneint

few mountain roads do transect the area, providing an opportunity to experience the roof of Snowdonia from the security of a vehicle.

WREXHAM

The tour begins in **Wrexham** ❶ at the town's most famous landmark,

Left: magnificent masonry and wood carvings within St Giles Church.

the 136ft (41m) Gothic tower of **St Giles Church** (Church St, daily 11am–3pm), which is considered one of the 'Seven Wonders of Wales'. The church you see today dates back to the 15th century and its interior contains fine stained glass, including a window attributed to Burne-Jones, and traces of a 15th-century wall painting of the Last Judgement. The town also has a museum (tel: 01978 297460; Mon–Fri 10am–5pm) and is the starting point for the Clywedog Trail, a 9-mile (14km) waymarked walking trail.

ERDDIG HALL

Leave Wrexham in a southerly direction on the A483, exit at junction 3, then follow signposts on minor roads to reach **Erddig Hall** ❷ (tel: 01978 355314; www.nationaltrust. org.uk; Mar–Oct daily 12.30–4.30pm, Nov–Feb limited tours only 11.30am–3.30pm daily). This 18th-century mansion, set in extensive grounds, offers a fascinating glimpse of the 'upstairs-downstairs' aspects of country-house life. In the family's grand rooms, visitors can see fine furniture, paintings and textiles, which contrast with the servants' quarters and kitchens 'below stairs'.

Ⓢ Wrexham's Markets

Every Monday in Wrexham there's a large outdoor market in Queen's Square, with stalls selling everything from fruit and vegetables to clothes and carpets. On the third Friday of each month, the square is the site of a Farmers' Market, where you can find great local food like beef, fish, cheese and preserves.

Above: Wrexham is home to North Wales' largest market.

CHIRK AND THE CEIRIOG VALLEY

Rejoin the A483 and continue heading south. After 7 miles (11km), at a roundabout, join the A5 towards Llangollen, then in a short distance join the B5070 to **Chirk**. Two miles (3km) west of Chirk, just beyond Chirk Station, is **Chirk Castle** ❸ (tel: 01691 777701; www.nationaltrust.org.uk;

Below: visit Erddig Hall for an insight into 18th-century country-house life.

Above: narrow boats and horse-drawn boats use Llangollen Canal.

state rooms end Feb–Mar and Oct daily noon–4pm, Apr–Sept until 5pm, Nov–Dec limited tours). It looks like a grand stately home, but was built around 1295, during the reign of Edward I and with his royal approval. Work finished around 1310. The castle changed hands several times until, in 1595, it was purchased by Sir Thomas Myddelton, a London merchant who made it into a comfortable family home. The state rooms boast the fine furniture and paintings you'd expect from a grand house, while the extensive parkland is well worth exploring.

From Chirk, you can opt to make a wonderfully scenic drive along the

B4500, which winds through the pastoral countryside of the **Ceiriog Valley** (Glyn Ceiriog). You can follow the road all the way to Llanarmon Dyffryn Ceiriog (bearing left on an unclassified road at The Hand public house, which includes an attractive inn). It's about 11 miles (18km) from Chirk. Return the same route to Chirk to rejoin the main drive and go west on the A5 to reach Llangollen.

LLANGOLLEN

Llangollen ❹ is a lively market town on the River Dee, surrounded by picturesque scenery. It's a popular centre for people on narrow-boat

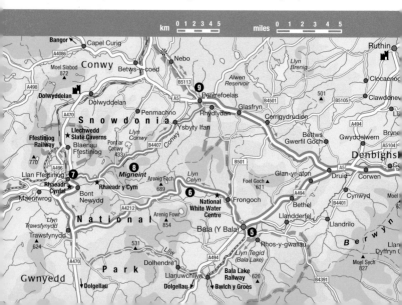

holidays, as the **Llangollen Canal** runs through town, part of Thomas Telford's Pontcysyllte Aqueduct. Railway fans will want to take a journey on the **Llangollen Railway** (tel: 01978 860979, timetable info 01978 860951; www.llangollen-railway.co.uk; most weekends all year, weekdays Apr–Oct) a steam railway which runs for 7½ miles (12km) from Llangollen station to Carrog, alongside the river.

PLAS NEWYDD

Llangollen's most famous sight is **Plas Newydd** (Hill Street; tel: 01978 862834; www.nationaltrust.org. uk; mid-Mar–Oct Sat–Wed noon–4.30pm), the former home of Sarah Ponsonby and Lady Eleanor Charlotte Butler, an 18th-century lesbian couple who eloped together, set up home and became known as the Ladies of Llangollen. They lived together for 50 years and became quite a tourist attraction in their lifetime, receiving distinguished visitors ranging from the Duke of Wellington and Sir Walter Scott to Josiah Wedgwood and William Wordsworth. Their house, a fairly simple cottage when they bought it, was transformed over the years into an overpowering Gothic creation, with lots of oak panelling and stained glass. Inside is an exhibition on their lives, while their bedchamber has been furnished to look much as it did at the end of their lives.

VALLE CRUCIS ABBEY

Around 1½ miles (2.5km) outside Llangollen, on the A542, are the romantic ruins of **Valle Crucis Abbey** (tel: 01978 860326; www.cadw.wales. gov.uk; Apr–end Oct 10am–5pm; open access rest of year), a Cistercian house founded in 1201. At that time this would have been an extremely isolated spot, ideal for contemplation. You can still feel the grandeur of the building, which was deserted after the Dissolution in the 16th century – and can even see the monks' fishpond.

Above: enthusiasts preserved and reopened the railway after its closure.

Above: ruins of Valle Crucis Abbey on the hill above Llangollen.

BALA

Take the A5 from Llangollen, driving through Corwen, shortly after which you turn left to join the A494 to reach **Bala ❺**, in Snowdonia National Park. Bala was a prosperous centre of the woollen industry prior to the Industrial Revolution. Thomas Pennant wrote of women and children 'in full employ, knitting along the roads'. But, the town's reputation as a religious centre proved more enduring. There is a statue to Thomas Charles, pioneer of Welsh Calvinistic Methodism and a leader of the Sunday School movement.

BALA LAKE

Bala Lake (Llyn Tegid) constitutes the largest natural area of water in Wales, being about 4 miles (6.4km) long by ¾ mile (1.2km) wide and with a maximum depth of around 136ft

Above: canoeing at the National White Water Centre.

(48m). Because of its situation in the great rift valley extending southwest to Tal-y-lyn and the sea at Tywyn – a natural through-route from the Vale of Chester – many travellers have written of the lake, its prodigious fish population (including the unique alpine gwyniad) and the fine sailing to be had upon its waters.

Hauled by narrow-gauge steam and diesel engines, the **Bala Lake Railway** (tel: 01678 540666; www. bala-lake-railway.co.uk; daily July–Aug, Apr–June and Sept check timetable) carries visitors for 9 miles (14km) along the scenic eastern shore of the lake between Bala and the village of Llanuwchllyn – the birthplace of Michael Jones, a prominent Welsh Nationalist who initiated Welsh settlement in Patagonia.

To the southeast of Llanuwchllyn, an impressive mountain road climbing to Bwlch y Groes is well worth the detour. This is Wales's highest road pass at 1,790ft (546m), giving access to the mighty Aran Mountains before dropping to Dinas Mawddwy (see Tour 8, p.96). A similarly high-level road heads west from Llanuwchllyn. At Pen-y-bont, 300yds/m after joining the northbound A494, turn left beside the Afon Lliw. In about 1½ miles (2.5km) the road crosses the river at Dolhendre and begins a long ascent into wild open country before recrossing the Afon Lliw to reach its

Above: Bala Lake, the largest natural area of water in the country, appeals to sailors and anglers.

highest point at 1,742ft (531m) above sea level. Travellers should note, however, that while spectacular, the route does involve the opening and closing of numerous gates. Passing through forestry and accompanying the Afon Gain for a mile (1.6km) or so lower down, the route swings northwest to meet the A470 near Trawsfynydd (*see Tour 6, p.78*).

NATIONAL WHITE WATER CENTRE

A much easier road to the west, also joining the A470 near Trawsfynydd, is the A4212 from Bala, via Llyn Celyn, a large reservoir. Just beyond the junc-

tion with the B4501 at Frongoch, to the left of the main road, is the **National White Water Centre** (tel: 01678 521083; www.ukrafting.co.uk), where, even if you don't want to do white-water rafting, you can enjoy their woodland walking trail, picnic spots or café beside the Afon Tryweryn. The centre also offers kayaking and canoeing.

A DROWNED VILLAGE

Not so many years ago **Llyn Celyn** ❻ itself was just a marshy valley containing the long-established community of Capel Celyn and the old railway line from Blaenau Ffestiniog

❺ From Wales to Patagonia

In the mid-19th century, as the pressure to speak English increased, moves were made to protect the language by moving overseas. A Welsh nationalist non conformist, Michael D. Jones, who lived near Bala, put forward the idea of establishing a community in Patagonia. He finally got together around 150 Welsh speakers, who left from Liverpool in 1865. The community still exists today.

Above: Welsh community members on their ranch in Patagonia.

Above: an isolated farmhouse in the heart of the Welsh upland moorland known as the Migneint (Swampy Place).

to Bala. During the 1960s – a time of momentous environmental decisions, not least the building of Trawsfynydd nuclear power station – the Afon Tryweryn was dammed to form Llyn Celyn as a holding reservoir for Liverpool Corporation. Despite much public opposition, the village of Capel Celyn, with its school, post office, chapel and farms, was drowned. Many of the community subsequently emigrated to Pennsylvania, and they and the village are remembered by a bronze plaque set on a boulder just beyond the grass-covered dam, and in a newly restored chapel at the lake's north-western end. There is fishing in the lake and a number of parking lay-bys off the A4212. Continue on this road to Llyn Trawsfynydd.

RHAEADR CYNFAL

A mile (1.6km) beyond the decommissioned nuclear power station on the shore of Llyn Trawsfynydd, turn right with the A470 towards **Llan Ffestiniog ⑦**, a large village of terraced stone houses situated some way south of the main slate quarries which take its name. Blaenau Ffestiniog lies 3 miles (5km) to the north (see Tour 3, p.46). From near the old railway station a footpath leads to the delightful **Rhaeadr Cynfal**, or Cynfal Falls. An-

other fine waterfall on the Afon Cynfal – Rhaeadr y Cwm – can be reached on foot 1½ miles (2.5km) upstream from Bont Newydd where the A470 bends sharply left to cross the river.

THE MIGNEINT

At Llan Ffestiniog turn right onto the B4391, the old, pre-power station road from Porthmadog to Bala. Soon after passing a superb viewpoint into the Cynfal ravine, take a left turn onto the B4407. In every direction the land rolls out into bog and heather moorland. This is the **Migneint ⑧** (Swampy Place). The often saturated hillsides of reeds and peat hags, where acid ground has encouraged the growth of mat-grass, cottongrass and deer's hair-sedge, represent the most significant area of such terrain in Wales. Walkers venturing forth have to contend with pools of black water, very soggy going and in all likelihood the need to navigate by compass in the frequent mists. Little wonder it is so little visited. Nevertheless, the Migneint is extremely important ecologically. Large tracts have been acquired by the National Trust and designated a Site of Special Scientific Interest.

The ribbon of tarmac winds over this desolate, lake-dotted wilderness, home to birds like golden plovers, snipe, grouse and curlew, and in about 3 miles (5km), at Pont ar Conwy, crosses the infant River Conwy not far from its source in Llyn Conwy. To the southeast rises the peak of Arenig Fach (2,261ft/689m), while downstream is the sleepy village of Ysbyty Ifan, centre of the National Trust's large Penrhyn Estate.

Fork right on an unclassified road over the River Conwy, continuing to **Pentrefoelas** ❾ on the A5. From here, on a clear day, visitors are strongly recommended to take a short detour to the north along the B5113. After the village of Nebo, the B5421 branches off to Llanrwst *(see Tour 1, p.23)*, but just beyond this fork in the road is a lay-by offering stunning views down into the Conwy Valley and up to the distant summits of Snowdonia.

Back on the A5, bypass Rhydlydan and continue to Cerrigydrudion. You may wish to extend this tour by turning right onto the B4501 Bala Road 1 mile (1.6km) south of the village. Once across the Afon Ceirw, this climbs over to the Afon Medrad valley before swinging west and south to Frongoch and back to Bala. Otherwise continue on the A5 to return to Llangollen, after which you bear north on the A483 to reach Wrexham again.

Ⓔ Eating Out

Nr Wrexham
Pant-yr-Ochain
Old Wrexham Road, Gresford; tel: 01978 853525; www.pantyrochain-gresford.co.uk; food served Mon–Sat noon–9.30pm, Sun until 9pm.
A lovely 16th-century manor house, set in pretty gardens, that is now an inn. The menu features dishes such as shoulder of lamb with dauphinoise potatoes, smoked haddock and salmon fish cakes, as well as good vegetarian options. Desserts might include summer pudding or Bakewell tart. ££

Llangollen
The Corn Mill
Dee Lane; tel: 01978 869555; www.cornmill-llangollen.co.uk; Mon–Sat noon–9.30pm, Sun until 9pm.
On fine days you can sit outside on the decked area beside the river at this lovely converted corn mill in Llangollen. As well as a good selection of light meals, you can enjoy local produce such as pork and leek sausages with mash, or chicken, ham hock and leek pie. Try the *bara brith* bread-and-butter pudding for dessert. ££

Nr Corwen
Tyddan Llan
Llandrillo; tel: 01490 440264; www.tyddynllan.co.uk, daily dinner 7–9pm, lunch Fri–Sun, booking essential.
The menu at this Michelin-starred restaurant, set in the countryside near Corwen, reflects the best of Welsh produce, and changes frequently. You might find fillet of turbot or duck breast with potato pancakes on the menu, with Wye Valley rhubarb and champagne trifle for dessert. There's also a tasting menu, and vegetarians can be catered for with notice. £££

Nr Chirk
The West Arms Hotel
Llanarmon Dyffyn-Ceiriog; tel: 01691 600665; www.thewestarms.co.uk; daily noon–9pm.
Sitting at the heart of the scenic Ceiriog Valley, this inn boasts plenty of atmosphere with log fires, low ceilings and a cosy bar. Bar meals include options such as a grilled Ceiriog trout or gammon steak with chips, while restaurant dishes might include Welsh black beef and poached pear and chocolate ganache for dessert. ££–£££

Snowdonia Nationa

Designated in 1951, the Snowdonia National Park sits in the anc
Gwynedd and covers 823 sq miles (2,132 sq km). Known as 'Eryr
the Park's most famous feature is its eponymous mountain, Snov

The National Park encompasses nine mountain ranges, with 90 peaks over 2,000ft (609m), and 15 over 3,000ft (914m). Add to these the many lakes, waterfalls, forests and soft green valleys – plus an extensive coastline etched with beaches of the softest sand – and you have a landscape of extraordinary variety. Snowdonia also has a complex geology, and fossil shell fragments found on the summit of Snowdon are a reminder that 500 million years ago the top of this mountain was part of the sea bed.

Snowdonia's wildlife is wonderfully rich, and some species are unique to the area – notably arctic alpine plants like the Snowdon lily, and the brightly coloured Snowdon beetle. In Llyn Tegid, the largest natural lake in the National Park, there's even a type of fish known as the gwyniad, which was trapped in the deep waters at the end of the last Ice Age and has evolved into a distinct subspecies.

RARE WILDLIFE

The lake is also home to the marvellously named glutinous snail, a freshwater snail that is one of the rarest

ark

h region of
Highland' in Welsh,

producing dark coloured pearls. Bird-watchers have the chance of spotting a wide variety of birds, ranging from black grouse and golden plovers to nightjars and skylarks. It is the range of habitats that is so important, and Snowdonia has precious woodlands and wetlands that are vital to many species. Dormice may be too small to see, but they inhabit the National Park, along with other mammals that are becoming increasingly rare in various parts of the UK – brown hares, pine martens and red squirrels.

PATHS, TRACKS AND TRAILS

The National Park is also a rich repository of Welsh culture, a land rich in myths and legends, where the Welsh language is widely spoken. It's a great place for getting out and about as it's laced with a seemingly endless number of walking and cycle routes: easy forest tracks, challenging mountain climbs, long-distance trails – there is something to suit everyone from families to fitness fanatics. Both walkers and cyclists can enjoy routes like the Mawddach Trail, a former railway line that runs for 9 miles (14km) between Dolgellau and Barmouth. Long-distance walks include the North Wales Path, a largely coastal trail stretching 60 miles (96km) from Prestatyn to Bangor, to the extremely challenging Cambrian Way (www.cambrianway.org.uk), which runs from Cardiff on the south coast, up through Snowdonia, over Snowdon and on to Conwy on the north coast. It's a lung-stretching 274 miles (483km) and not for the faint-hearted.

For more information on the Snowdonia National Park, check out www.eryri-npa.gov.uk or go into one of the National Park Information Centres in Betws-y-coed, Beddgelert, Harlech, Dolgellau and Aberdyfi.

in Europe. Other invertebrates to be found in Snowdonia include several butterflies: the small silver-studded blue, the glorious gold and orange-hued marsh fritillary, and the large heath butterfly.

There is a fragile population of freshwater pearl mussels as well. These little mussels, which like to live in fast-running cool water, can live for up to 100 years and are noted for

Above: Mount Snowdon. **Top Left:** one of the footpaths winding up Snowdon through slate scree. **Centre Left:** the B4391 crossing the Migneint. **Left**: insignia on a Snowdon Mountain Railway carriage.

Tour 8

Dolgellau to Cadair Idris and the Aran Mountains

This tour of around 40 miles (64km) brings you close to the mysterious peak of Cadair Idris and at a relaxed pace can take a whole day

This tour starts at Dolgellau which, slightly offset from the great Bala–Tal y Llyn geological fault line, stands near the southern entrance to the Snowdonia National Park. Apart from Cadair Idris, Snowdon's equivalent in the popularity stakes, less familiar country stretches southeast to the beautiful valley of the River Dyfi (often anglicised to Dovey). The vast Dyfi Forest, threaded by old slate-mining tracks, spreads its mantle of conifers over a complex, folded landscape. Some of the hilltops sport wind turbines, for this is 'alternative technology' territory. To the east of Dolgellau, the volcanic Aran mountains extend from Dinas Mawddwy to

Highlights

- Dolgellau
- Cadair Idris
- Centre for Alternative Technology
- Dinas Mawddwy
- Bwlch y Groes
- Coed-y-Brenin

Bala Lake, only failing by a whisker to reach the magic 3,000ft (915m) but nevertheless boasting Wales's highest road. To the north lies the Coed-y-Brenin Forest, where larch and Sitka spruce clothe a hilly landscape whose streams all flow into the Mawddach; it is an area of waterfalls, abandoned

F Our Lady of Sorrows

On Meyrick Street in Dolgellau is Our Lady of Sorrows Church. It opened in the 1960s, thanks to a Maltese priest Francis Scalpell who had come here in 1939 and started to celebrate Mass in a former stable. With the help of Italian POWs he built a rudimentary church, but was determined to have a more permanent structure. Eventually he raised the necessary funds and this church is the result.

Above: Father Scalpell contributed to the architect's design for the church.

gold and copper mines and numerous forest trails, ideal for walkers and mountain bikers.

DOLGELLAU

The tour starts in **Dolgellau** ❶ which has for centuries provided hospitality for travellers and it remains a great favourite with visitors today. In the early 1400s, Owain Glyndwr assembled a parliament here, while in the 19th century it briefly became a hub of activity when gold was discovered in the surrounding rocks. However, the town's main significance revolved around its great sheep and cattle fairs. Livestock are still brought in for the weekly market and there is a major summer agricultural show. The town's mostly 19th-century Market Square area of pale granite buildings is less bothered by traffic than it once was thanks to the road by pass, but it is still a busy place. Narrow, irregular streets lined with shops and restaurants invite browsing, while to the north, not far from the Parish Church with its medieval tower and excellent Victorian stained glass,

Above Left: Coed-y-Brenin forest is a prime location for mountain biking with its novice and technical trails.

a seven-arched bridge, **Bont Fawr**, spans the Afon Wnion.

The National Centre for Welsh Folk Music, **Ty Siamas** (tel: 01341 421800; www.tysiamas.com), is located in a former market hall in the town centre. There's a café/bar and a shop, as well as an exhibition. Live

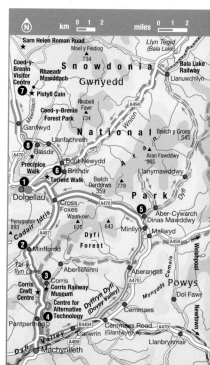

G A Circuit of Dolgellau

From Dolgellau you can follow the Glyn Aran walk, a 2½-mile (4km) circular walk that gives you great views both of the town and of the peaks of Cadair Idris. From the path you can see a farmhouse, Bryn Mawr, which belonged to Rowland Ellis, a Quaker, in the 17th century. He led a group of Quakers to Pennsylvania, where they built a replica farmhouse, which later gave its name to a town.

performances are staged throughout the year, as well as multimedia presentations on folk music.

CADAIR IDRIS

Follow the A470 east up to Cross Foxes and bear right onto the A487. High mountain country lies ahead, and from the pass (Bwlch Talyllyn) at 938ft (286m) there are stunning views down the crag-bound upper valley here on the Bala–Talyllyn fault line (the largest land-shift in Wales) running northeast to southwest through southern Snowdonia. Tal-y-Llyn Lake gleams in the distance, while up to the right rear the outlying flanks of **Cadair Idris**

(Chair of Idris). This volcanic massif, eroded by aeons of glacial action into a peak of savage beauty, is named after Idris, a local hero killed in battle against the Saxons around AD 630. Tradition decrees that anyone sleeping overnight in the 'chair' (its precise position is unclear) will wake as either a lunatic or a poet.

You can park at **Minffordd ❷** to follow the **Minffordd Path** (6 miles/ 9.6km return) for an ascent of Cadair

Above: Dolgellau's buildings were constructed using local granite.
Below: Bont Fawr, Dolgellau's seven-arched bridge.

Right: Cadair Idris. **Below**: take a train ride and explore the old engine shed at Corris' Railway Museum.

Idris from the south. This route goes via the lovely Llyn Cau to Penygadair, 2,929ft (893m), Cadair Idris's highest top, but although it's probably the shortest route up the mountain it's also the hardest, with an ascent of 2,850ft (869m). It's a rough climb, as serious as Snowdon – but without trains or a café on top. Interestingly, during the late 19th century one Richard Pugh of Dolgellau did construct a stone hut on the summit in which he provided visitors with 'all convenient refreshments while waiting for the dispersion of the misty clouds in order to enjoy the exquisite prospect...' Pugh's hut remains, now down graded to a basic shelter but welcome nonetheless. (For Cadair Idris from the north, see *Tour 9, p.100*.)

Less than a mile (1.3km) southwest of Minffordd on the B4405, cradled by sweeping mountainsides, stretch the waters of Tal-y-llyn Lake (or, to give it its true Welsh name, Llyn Mwyngil – Lake in the Pleasant Retreat). It is indeed a peaceful lake, shallow but abundant in fish and flora, notably its yellow water-lily. From the handsome Tyn y Cornel Hotel, and the adjacent little unspoilt church, a lakeside track along the north shore provides an easy and pleasant walk to Minffordd.

CORRIS

The A487 Machynlleth road continues towards Corris, but most visitors first call at **Corris Craft Centre** (www. corriscraftcentre.co.uk), a purpose-built, modernist complex of studios in which crafts people can be observed making pottery, toys, leatherware, jewellery and candles. There is also a restaurant and **King Arthur's Labyrinth** (tel: 01654 761584; www.king arthurslabyrinth.co.uk; end Mar–Oct daily 10am–5pm). Access is by boat through a magic waterfall to subterranean caverns where you then walk underground, while some of the Welsh legends pertaining to King Arthur are explored in tableaux with light and sound effects.

The town of **Corris ❸**, east off the main road, stands amidst the convoluted, timber-clad hills of Dyfi Forest. The village grew up around slate quarrying in the Afon Dulas valley, and a narrow-gauge railway was built in 1859 to transport slate down to the main line at Machynlleth. Steam locomotives replaced horses in 1879. For more details of this and the Corris Railway Society's restoration work, visit the **Railway Museum** (tel: 01654 761303; www.corris. co.uk; Apr–Oct 10.30am–5pm when trains operate, check timetable first).

A 50-minute round trip on the train includes a guided tour of the sheds.

As well as a Heritage Trail north of the village, there are forest trails suitable for walking and cycling further up the Dulas valley around Aberllefenni.

CENTRE FOR ALTERNATIVE TECHNOLOGY

Signed to the left off a bend in the descending A487 road is one of southern Snowdonia's most compelling visitor attractions. The **Centre for Alternative Technology ❹** (CAT; tel: 01654 705950; www.cat.org.uk; Apr–Oct daily 10am–5pm, Nov–Mar until dusk) was developed from modest beginnings in the early 1970s at a disused slate quarry near the hamlet of Pantperthog. Its ethos is to demonstrate the effectiveness of alternative energy sources, house insulation and organic food production.

By examining such technologies as solar, wind and wave power, house building and sustainable soil fertilisation, the centre challenges conventional views in a thought-provoking

and entertaining way about how an advanced industrial society should utilise its resources. It would be easy to spend a whole day here, and it's a great attraction for all ages. Entry is by water-powered cliff railway, and within the 7 acres (2.8 hectares) can be found hands-on displays, organic gardens, animals and beehives, a vegetarian restaurant, a bookshop and more. There is even an electric vehicle charge point for visitors arriving by electric car.

DYFI VALLEY

Both the main A487 road and a parallel lane on the east bank of the Afon Dulas descend into the lovely Dovey Valley or Dyffryn Dyfi. Traditionally the frontier between north and south Wales, this is the modern-day meeting place of Gwynedd, Powys and Ceredigion. Across the Afon Dyfi stands Machynlleth, a colourful, bustling market town with many interesting features (see Tour 9, p.108).

Turn left on the B4404 past Llanwrin and stay on the northwest bank of the Dyfi on an unclassified road all the way to Aberangell and Minllyn, small

Left: pick up practical ideas on how to live a more sustainable lifestyle at the Centre for Alternative Technology. **Right**: Dyfi Forest and Valley.

villages on the eastern fringe of Dyfi Forest. On the skyline of Mynydd y Cemais to the southeast are ranged wind turbines belonging to the CAT's wind farm. The road closely shadows the dismantled Mawddwy Railway which, in the mid-19th century, connected Dinas Mawddwy with the main Cambrian Railway at Cemmaes Road 7 miles (11km) to the south. Passenger services ceased in 1930 but the line was kept open for goods traffic until damage to a bridge over the Dyfi closed it more conclusively in 1951.

Ever-industrious, the Victorians had planned to extend the Mawddwy line north to join the Great Western Railway at Llanuwchllyn (see Tour 3, p.47) by tunnelling beneath the Aran mountains. Unfortunately the plan was never realised as the project's sponsor, local landowner Sir Edmund Buckley, was declared bankrupt in 1876 before work began.

On the outskirts of Dinas Mawddwy on the A470 near Pont Minllyn, a 17th-century packhorse bridge, stands **Meirion Mill** (tel: 01650 531311; www. meirionmill.co.uk; Apr–Oct Mon–Sat 10am–5pm, Sun 10.30am–5pm, Nov–Mar Mon–Sat 10am–4.30pm, Sun 10.30am–4.30pm), a craft and clothing shop set in the old Dinas Mawddwy station buildings.

Ⓕ The Tudors

After Edward I's brutal conquest of Wales, there was a distinct irony in the fact that, in 1485 at the Battle of Bosworth, an English king (Richard III) was beaten by a Welshman, Henry Tudor, who gained the throne and became Henry VII. Henry ensured that Welshmen were rewarded with positions of power at court. However, his son, Henry VIII, put an end to Welsh independence by instituting the Acts of Union of 1536 and 1542. Although these gave the Welsh legal equality, they introduced English law to Wales and made English the language of the courts.

Above: Henry Tudor was born in Pembroke Castle.

Above: Dinas Mawddwy. Local walks vary from gentle strolls along fairly level paths to tackling the Aran Ridge.

DINAS MAWDDWY

Dinas Mawddwy ❺ itself was described by George Borrow in *Wild Wales* (published in 1862) as 'little more than a collection of filthy huts… Fierce-looking red-haired banditti of old were staggering about, and sounds of drunken revelry echoed from the huts…' Dinas, however, had once been a much more important place, with over 1,000 inhabitants, shops, inns, several fairs and major cattle sales. Later prosperity came from lead mining and slate quarrying. Today the village, snug in an amphitheatre of wooded and rhododendron-clad hills at the confluence of the Dyfi and Cerist rivers, enjoys a more peaceful existence as a walking centre.

BWLCH Y GROES

To the north lie the volcanic Aran Mountains, which extend to Bala Lake and culminate in Aran Fawddwy (2,969ft/905m). To explore the Aran ridge, drive northeast to Aber-Cywarch and there turn left to Cwm Cywarch. Following access problems in the 1980s, the Arans are regaining their popularity, but keep to the

Above: a head for heights is needed for the Precipice Walk.

THE TORRENT WALK AND PRECIPICE WALK

A direct return to Dolgellau from Dinas Mawddwy can be made on the A470. Ascending the Cerist valley to Bwlch Oerddrws (Cold Door Pass) at 1,178ft (359m), it skirts scenic cwms and waterfalls. Beyond the pass there are magnificent views of Cadair Idris.

After passing Cross Foxes once again, about 2½ miles (4km) before reaching Dolgellau, turn sharp right onto the B4416 to **Brithdir** ❻. Half a mile (0.8km) before the village, a path opposite St Mark's Church marks the start of the popular **Torrent Walk**. About 2½ miles (4km) in length, the path's best stretch drops through beautiful deciduous woodland beside a series of waterfalls in the fast-flowing Afon Clywedog.

Continue on the B4416 to Bont Newydd, cross the junction with the A494, and follow the narrow, twisting lane to the tiny settlement of Llanfachreth. (A wider unclassified road reaches here from Dolgellau via the slopes of Foel Offrwm.)

The best-known **Precipice Walk**, and the first to be established in the Snowdonia region, begins southwest of Llanfachreth from roadside car parking (Saithgroesffordd), where the road forks for Ty'n Groes. Much of the 3-mile (5km) circular walk, which takes in lovely Llyn Cynwch and stunning views over the Mawddach estuary, is easy and intrinsically safe. In places, however, it does traverse very steep hillside. The path is not a public right of way, instead enjoying concessionary status since 1890, courtesy of the Nannau Estate.

COED-Y-BRENIN

Llanfachreth nestles at the southern edge of the magnificent Coed-y-Brenin (The King's Forest), so named after George V's Silver Jubilee

concessionary paths and heed the 'No Dogs' signs. Being properly equipped and choosing favourable weather become even more vital in remote hills such as these. As a detour to the route, the unclassified mountain road continues beside the Afon Dyfi to Llanymawddwy, shortly beyond which the river is crossed and the scenery grows appreciably wilder by the minute. Precipitous slopes up to 1,000ft (300m) high, deeply scarred by stream beds, crowd in ahead. The road is correspondingly steep as it climbs the tributary valley of the Afon Rhiwlech, passes a right fork to Lake Vyrnwy and reaches **Bwlch y Groes**, 1,788ft (545m) above sea level. There is car parking here at Wales's highest road pass and views extend north towards the Arenig mountains and west to the Arans – a truly spectacular spot to be attained by vehicle. The road descends to Llanuwchllyn, not far from the southern end of Bala Lake (see Tour 7, p.84), from where you can join the A494 back to Dolgellau.

Left: Bwlch y Groes is also known as Hellfire Pass.

Left: explore Coed-y-Brenin forest on foot or by bike – there are walking and cycling trails specifically for families.

GLASDIR

At **Glasdir** ❽ less than a mile (1.6km) west of Llanfachreth on the banks of the tumbling Afon Las, an Arboretum of mountain tree species has been established. Further down still are the ruins of **Glasdir Copper Mine**, which you can explore on a short walking trail from Glasdir. The copper mine opened in 1852, however; the mineral, present in the rocks and impregnated peat of the Mawddach valley, had probably been extracted since prehistoric times. At the height of its activity, Glasdir Mine, worked by some 160 employees, produced 50 tons of ore per day. The mine finally closed in 1914.

From Glasdir take the left-hand of two parallel lanes dropping to the Afon Wen and cross the river near its confluence with the Afon Eden. In under a mile (1.6km) this forestry by road crosses the Afon Eden and joins the A470. Ahead at Ganllwyd there is car parking for a short walk west up to Rhaeadr Du and a sequence of beautiful waterfalls in the Afon Gamlan.

WATERFALLS

At the end of the adopted road beside the infant Afon Mawddach northeast from Ganllwyd (to the east of the A470), a rough track (no vehicles) continues to Bont Gwynfynydd. Here the rivers Mawddach and Gain each roar over their own spectacular waterfalls – Rhaeadr Mawddach and Pistyll Gain respectively – before joining forces near the site of the old Gwynfynydd Gold Mine. The now derelict mine, which had closed in 1939, was temporarily resurrected in the 1980s, and again in the 1990s.

in 1935. Despite impressive commercial statistics (yielding thousands of tons of timber annually), Coed-y-Brenin remains one of the most varied and lovely forests in Wales. Situated in what used to be Meirioneth, it straddles the rivers Gamlan, Eden, Gain and Wen, along with the Mawddach into which all the others flow. Within the forest can be found wooded gorges, crags, waterfalls and boulder-strewn rivers, secluded upland pastures and a scattering of farmsteads.

Stunning views can be enjoyed from the café and restaurant at the **Coed-y-Brenin Visitor Centre** ❼ (tel: 01341 440747; summer Mon–Fri 9.30am–5pm, Sat–Sun 9am–5pm, winter until 4.30pm). Situated to the east of the A470, 8 miles (13km) north of Dolgellau, the Centre also has cycle hire, showers and a children's playground. Pick up details of the many waymarked walking and mountain-biking forest trails; it is possible to plan delightful rambles or mountain-bike tours from any of the numerous car parks and picnic areas.

However, stocks of the metal have now disappeared – it is so rare it fetches three times the price of ordinary gold. Pure Welsh gold bears the 'Welsh Maiden' mark and the hallmark 'Aur Cymru'.

Parallel to the A470 for some distance to the east, lies the course of Sarn Helen, an ancient north-to-south Roman road (though most went east towards Offa's Dyke). It was adapted by the Romans for their own use to link Caerhun, near Conwy (see Tour 1, p.20), with Maridunum (Carmarthen) and can still be traced, intermittently, throughout the entire length of Wales. According to the Mabinogion, a collection of mythical stories dating back to the 13th century, the road was laid in the 4th century AD by Helen, noble bride of the self-styled Emperor Magnus Maximus who was dream-led to Wales by his vision of her.

ⓔ Eating Out

Dolgellau
Y Merionnydd
Smithfield Square; tel: 01341 422554; www.themeirionnydd.com; Tue–Sat from 6.30pm; other days and times vary with the seasons, telephone to check.
This hotel restaurant, in a fine old stone building in Dolgellau, offers a regularly changing menu of modern British dishes, with plenty of Welsh produce. Lamb shank, fish and beef feature frequently, and there are always vegetarian options. ££

Y Sospan
Queen's Square; tel: 01341 423174; www.ysospan.co.uk; daily, café 9am–5pm, bistro 6–9pm.
The downstairs café offers light meals and snacks like baguettes and lasagne, while the upstairs restaurant has a changing menu that might feature starters of crab cakes, and mains such as orange and rosemary lamb, chicken supreme or venison steak, as well as several vegetarian options. There's a separate children's menu available. £–££

Nr Llanelltyd
The Eagles Inn
Llanuwchllyn; tel: 01678 540278; www.theeagleinn-bala.co.uk; summer daily noon–2.30pm and 6–9.30pm, winter Thur–Sun noon–2.30pm and 6–9.30pm, Mon–Wed dinner only.

This pub in the little village of Llanuwchllyn serves real ales and a good selection of bar meals ranging from a mixed grill to lamb burgers or ham, egg and chips. There are several vegetarian options, such as goats' cheese soufflé, and a children's menu. £

The Brigands Inn
Mallwyd; tel: 01650 511999, www.brigandsinn.com; food served daily, 8am–9pm.
This restored 15th-century coaching inn has a regularly changing lunch and dinner menu, and also offers breakfast in the mornings, and light meals in the afternoons. Typical dishes might be pork belly or gourmet burger and chips, with vegetarian choices like vegetable tagine. Desserts are home-made and delicious. £–££

Mawddach
Llanelltyd, by the A470 outside Dolgellau; tel: 01341 421752; www.mawddach.com; lunch Wed–Sun noon–2.30pm, dinner Thur–Sat 6.30–9pm.
This Michelin-recommended restaurant is in a sleek, contemporary bar conversion with views of Cadair Idris and the Mawddach estuary. The lunch menu features dishes such as asparagus risotto and Welsh Black rib burger with triple-cooked chips. A traditional Sunday lunch is also available. ££

Tour 9

Cadair Idris to Machynlleth

This 48-mile (77km) full-day tour takes you past the peaks of Cadair Idris, then along the Cardigan coast, before heading back inland to the ancient town of Machynlleth

Between the Mawddach and the Dyfi (Dovey) estuaries lies a bulge of high land rising to Cadair Idris and split through the middle by the Bala–Talyllyn geological fault. Mountain roads probe the heart of this, the Snowdonia National Park's most southerly outpost with its ancient churches, castle ruins, 'Great Little Trains' and links with the legend of King Arthur. At Fairbourne, Tywyn and Aberdyfi, long sandy beaches provide the setting for holiday activities without the razzmatazz of more commercially developed resorts. With the southern flanks of Cadair Idris examined in Tour 8 (see p.90), this route sees what the great mountain has to offer from the north and east, alternating between coast and foothills to

Highlights

- Cadair Idris
- Cregennen Lakes
- Fairbourne Steam Railway
- Castell y Bere
- Talyllyn Railway
- Aberdyfi
- Machynlleth

arrive, ultimately, at Machynlleth, the southernmost gateway to Snowdonia and a town with a rich Welsh history.

CADAIR IDRIS

This route starts in **Dolgellau ❶** (see Tour 8, p.91). Many come to this attractive town to explore the landscape around **Cadair Idris**, the mountain

Left: hiking in the Cadair Idris mountain range. **Right**: footpath around Cregennen Lakes.

range whose craggy northern escarpment dominates the horizon. Some come to climb its peaks, though it can be rough walking. Already by the mid-18th century, guides were leading visitors to the 2,927ft (893m) summit of Penygadair, the highest peak on the Cadair Idris range. Nowadays so many tramp up the mountain that footpath erosion is causing serious problems.

Fork left up the old coaching road, a narrow lane which leaves Dolgellau from the west end of Fford Cader Idris (Cadair Idris Street), and in 1 mile (1.6km) turn right to pass roadside Llyn Gwernan. The well-known **Fox's Path** up Cadair Idris starts here, but

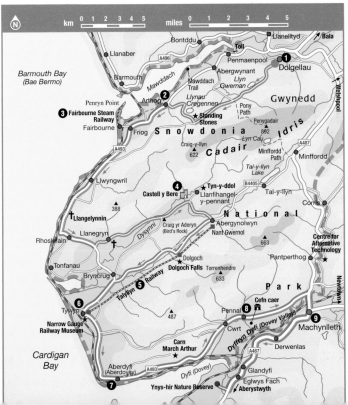

is now so badly eroded that it is no longer recommended. Further on at the Ty-nant car park at Pont Dyf-frydan is the official start of the Pony Path over to Cwm Pennant; from the saddle at its highest point (Rhiw Gwredydd), Cadair Idris's highest peak, Penygadair, is easily reached.

CREGENNEN LAKES

The road meanders along beneath frowning cliffs rising almost 1,500ft (450m) to Craig-las. About 300yds/m after crossing a cattle grid, turn off right to enjoy the two idyllically situated **Cregennen lakes** (Llynau Cregennen), which are popular with trout fishermen. They occupy part of a 705-acre (285-hectare) National Trust property donated in 1959 by Major C.L. Wynne-Jones in memory of his two sons killed in World War II. Standing stones marked on the Ordnance Survey map date from around 1800 BC; as with others in Snowdonia their exact purpose is unknown, but they might have been deity symbols,

or boundary or route markers. The heights of Cadair Idris loom to the east, with the Mawddach estuary stretching below to the west: glorious views of both can be had from the summit of the easily climbed hill immediately to the north of the lakes. The name 'Cregennen' is said to derive from 'crog-gangen', which means 'hanging branch'. Criminals were often hung from an oak tree in this area.

Right: a country lane winds past houses in Arthog. The Mawddach Trail passes near the village.

Left: Cregennen Lakes contain blue, rainbow and wild brown trout. **Right**: the owners of the Graig Wen campsite and Yurt at Arthog.

ARTHOG

A tortuous descent ensues to reach **Arthog ❷**. Waterfalls punctuate the stream flowing down through the village; few would guess that it rises in the tiniest of glacial corrie lakes – Llyn Cyri – high under Cadair Idris's outlying crags. Passing near Arthog, a 9-mile (15km) -long nature trail, established by the RSPB and the North Wales Naturalists' Trust, utilises the trackbed of the old Aberystwyth and Welsh Coast Railway (1865–1965). Called the **Mawddach Trail** (see *Tour 6, p.76*), it skirts the estuary's very shoreline and is suitable for walking or cycling. The route runs between Dolgellau and Barmouth. There is also a **circular walk** of 9 miles (14km) from Arthog that takes you into the hills. It runs through woodland that is a Site of Special Scientific Interest (SSSI), which has stunning displays of bluebells in spring, and goes past a 200-year-old beech tree and the remains of a 12th-century courtroom.

From Arthog, the road runs to **Fairbourne**, a settlement of mostly modern bungalows, which is home to the fascinating **Fairbourne Steam Railway ❸** (tel: 01341 250362; www.fairbournerailway.com; Easter–autumn daily; but check timetable for details) The railway runs over a mile (1.6km) out along a duney sandspit to Penrhyn Point. Dating back to 1895 and horse-drawn until 1916, the railway was originally a narrow-gauge conveyance of building materials. From the route, glorious river and mountain

Ⓕ King Arthur

Was King Arthur a Welshman? Many people think so and claim that his last battle was fought at Camlan in Snowdonia. Others think it was fought on Snowdon itself and that Llyn Llydaw, a lake at the foot of the mountain, was the stretch of water across which the dying king was rowed to reach the island of Avalon. In Welsh, his name, Arth Fawr, means the Great Bear, and some think he was a Celtic god. Others consider it more likely that he was a 5th-century Celtic chieftain who fought against the Saxons.

Above: Arthur and Merlin receive Excalibur from the Lady of the Lake.

ⓖ Walks up Cadair Idris

There are three maintained routes up Cadair Idris. The toughest is the Minffordd Path, which starts from Dol Idris car park after the junction of the A487 and B4405 Dolgellau to Tywyn road. It's a 6-mile (9.6km) return route. The Pony Path, which is a similar distance, starts from the car park at Ty Nant farm, and is the classic ascent offering the best views. The Llanfihangel-y-pennant Path is the longest route at 10 miles (16km) return, but the easiest walk. It starts in Llanfihangel-y-pennant.

Above: walking boots, water and waterproof clothing are essential.

views can be enjoyed and there is a seasonal foot-passenger ferry across to Barmouth (see Tour 6, p.75). An alternative crossing of the estuary can be made on the Cambrian Coast railway viaduct which has a pedestrian walkway (see Tour 5, p.65).

LLWYNGWRIL

One and three-quarter miles (3km) beyond **Llwyngwril** on the A493 coast road, adjacent to a railway halt, stands **Llangelynnin Church**. Set just above the shingle beach, this primitive, mainly 12th-century building is dedicated to a local 7th-century saint, Celynnin, and sits on the site of a much earlier structure. The church features some wall paintings, includ-

ing the Ten Commandments written in Welsh, and medieval gravestones inscribed in both Welsh and English can be found in the graveyard. Near the church is a Holy Well, the waters of which were once thought to heal sick children.

LLANEGRYN CHURCH

Heading south, high coastal hills force the A493 inland although the railway manages to squeeze past. In less than 2 miles (3km) bear left to **Llanegryn**, notable for another little church. This one sits on a hillside half a mile (800m) northwest of the village and reveals a remarkably beautiful rood screen and loft, probably carved by local craftsmen in the 15th or early 16th centuries, or, as tradition has it, brought there from Cymer Abbey near Dolgellau (see Tour 6, p.78) during the Reformation.

CASTELL Y BERE

The Afon Dysynni is crossed opposite the dramatic, soaring buttress of Craig yr Aderyn (Birds' Rock), the only inland cormorant nesting site in Britain. Straight over the crossroads, in a wild and romantic setting at the heart of mountainous country and with fabulous views of the western flanks of Cadair Idris, stand the extensive but fragmentary ruins of **Castell y Bere** ❹ (open at all times), an example of a native Welsh (rather than Norman or Edwardian) castle. Started by Llewellyn the Great around 1221, the fortress guarded southern Meirionydd and the mountain route to Dolgellau. During the early part of 1283 Castell y Bere became one of Prince Dafydd ap Gruffydd's final refuges but was eventually surrendered later that same year to Edward I's 3,000-strong invading army. It was the last Welsh castle to fall, and although it was briefly retaken, it was eventually destroyed and left to the elements.

LLANFIHANGEL-Y-PENNANT

At the road's end beyond **Llanfihangel-y-pennant**, a monument to Mary Jones has been installed in the ruin of her cottage, Tyn-y-ddol. In 1800, aged only 16, she walked barefoot over to Bala (about 26 miles/42km) to buy a Welsh Bible from the Methodist minister there, Thomas Charles *(see Tour 7, p.84).* He had none to sell but gave her his own. Mary's zeal for the scriptures so impressed him that he began a campaign, from which grew the British and Foreign Bible Society. From the adjacent road-end you can join the Pony Path for the classic ascent over the shoulder of Cadair Idris and on to Dolgellau.

TALYLLYN RAILWAY

Return to the crossroads and bear left to **Abergynolwyn**. Once an important slate quarrying centre, the village nestles in the Dysynni valley surrounded by forestry. Here, short of Tal-y-llyn lake itself, stands Nant Gwernol Station (forest walks but no road access), northern terminus of the famous

Above: the Talyllyn Railway train, pausing at Abergynolwyn station, has been running since 1865.

2ft 3in (68cm) narrow-gauge **Talyllyn Railway** ❺ (tel: 01654 710472; www.talyllyn.co.uk; daily end Mar–Nov but check timetable for details). The line is the oldest of its kind in the world and one of the best known of Wales's 'Great Little Trains'. In continuous service since 1865, originally used to transport slate to the main line at Tywyn down on the coast, its trains now merrily puff the 7¼ miles (11.6km) between Nant Gwernol and

Above: the ruins of Castell y Bere. Welsh castles were not usually as sophisticated as English ones: Welsh princes had less money.

Above: as well as its plethora of watersports and outdoor bound activities, Aberdyfi is the starting point for two long walks. **Right**: on Aberdyfi's pier.

Tywyn with cargoes of sightseers. The line was saved from obscurity in 1951 by the Tal-y-llyn Railway Preservation Society, the world's first such organisation, which has since been emulated by many similar groups. The entire railway journey of an hour each way can be varied by alighting at intermediate stations. A short walk from Dolgoch Station, for example, leads through woods to the attractive **Dolgoch Falls**; below the falls the line is carried across the little gorge on an impressive viaduct. There are also forest walks in the Nant Gwernol ravine.

TYWYN

Running parallel to the railway, the B4405 meets the A493 at Bryncrug, 2 miles (3km) from **Tywyn ⑥**. This is where the railway's main station is situated, together with the **Narrow Gauge Railway Museum** (tel: 01654 710472; www.ngrm.org.uk; Apr–Nov from 10am, Dec–Mar times vary), which combines displays of old locomotives with the history of the slate mining industry in North and Mid Wales. The museum has a section devoted to the Rev. W.V. Awdry, the

creator of Thomas the Tank Engine. Rev Awdry was once a volunteer on the Tal-y-llyn Railway. Tywyn's evolution as a seaside resort owed much to John Corbett, a salt baron from Droitwich who built Marine Terrace, the Market Hall and the Assembly Rooms (now a cinema). Adjacent to the latter stands St Cadfan's Church, in which will be found the 7th-century St Cadfan's Stone bearing an inscription thought to be the oldest example of written Welsh in existence.

ABERDYFI

Dunes seaward of the road and railway extend south to **Aberdyfi ⑦** (Aberdovey – meaning Mouth of the Dovey), a pleasant resort best known for its golf course and sailing facilities. There is a small Maritime Museum at the Tourist Information Centre on The Wharf (Easter–Oct daily). Started during World War I, it documents the little port's heritage of mineral exports, shipbuilding and seafaring. Aberdyfi boasts a major Outward Bound Centre and is popular with windsurfers, kitesurfers and sailors. Aberdyfi is also the starting point for the 108-mile (174km) **Dyfi Valley Way** exploring countryside on both flanks of the river north to its source under Aran Fawddwy, and crossing the site of King Arthur's legendary last battle at Camlan. The Dyfi is the traditional frontier between North and South Wales. The **Meirionnydd Coast Walk** also starts at Aberdyfi,

the route passing standing stones and holy wells as it takes you along the coast to Porthmadog. The path is 72 miles (116km) long and can be split into eight easy one-day sections.

Aberdyfi's profile was raised when Charles Dibdin composed the song *The Bells of Aberdovey* for his opera *Liberty Hall* in 1785. Of many stories surrounding the mysteriously pealing bells beneath the sea, the most commonly quoted (and embellished) concerns Cantre'r Gwaelod – the Lowland Hundred. This once fertile low-lying plain was protected from the sea by dykes in the care of Seithennin, a notorious drunkard. One stormy night, while making merry at a feast, he forgot to close the sluices. The Lowland Hundred was inundated and Manua, its principal settlement containing the bells, disappeared for ever beneath the waters of Cardigan Bay.

CARN MARCH ARTHUR

From the top of the village an unclassified road climbs to the route of a prehistoric ridgeway. Ten minutes'

F Owain Glyndwr

Owain Glyndwr (*c*.1350–1416) is a name you will hear wherever you travel in North Wales. Descended from the Princes of Powys, Glyndwr was wealthy and educated, and even served in the English army. When a nobleman in Ruthin appropriated some of his land, Glyndwr appealed to the courts but lost his case: the nobleman was close to Henry IV. Glyndwr gathered supporters and attacked Ruthin, the start of a rebellion against English rule. He took castles, including Harlech, and proclaimed the first Welsh parliament in Machynlleth in 1404. However, by 1408 when Harlech was taken

Above: the Owain Glyndwr Centre in Machynlleth.

by royal forces, he was forced into hiding somewhere in Snowdonia and vanished into obscurity. No one even knows where he is buried.

walk beyond the farm at the road-end is **Carn March Arthur**, a rock that is said to bear the hoofprint of King Arthur's horse, made as he leaped from a cliff to escape advancing Saxons. It's marked by a stone tablet. A little further on, to the left, lies Llyn Barfog (Bearded Lake), perhaps referring to its covering of water-lilies, or alternatively to tales of hairy monsters associated with Arthurian legend.

PENNAL

Tracing the Dyfi's shoreline (the National Park boundary), the A493 passes **Pennal** ❽. Pennal is an ancient site, and its church, **St Peter ad Vincula**, was founded in the 6th century. It was here, in 1406, that Owain Glyndwr is thought to have signed a letter to Charles VI of France asking for help in his rebellion and outlining his plans for an independent Wales, which included establishing Welsh universities, an independent church and a Welsh government. In the letter, known today as the Pennal Letter, Glyndwr offers to recognise Benedict XIII of Avignon as Pope – a concession he hoped would enlist French support. Today the church holds a facsimile of the letter. At Cefn caer, 1,640ft (500m) to the southeast, the Romans built a fort guarding one of the lowest crossing points on the Dyfi. A medieval hall house stands on the site (tel: 01654 791230; www.cefncaer.com; open to visitors by appointment). The house, which was home to Owain Glyndwr for a time, contains many original features. Nearby are the mounds of a Bronze Age tumulus and a medieval motte.

MACHYNLLETH

At Pen-y-bont turn right over the river and beneath the railway line to enter **Machynlleth** ❾. The town's centrepiece is a splendid Victorian Clock Tower built in 1873 to commemorate the Marquess of Londonderry's family who then owned the imposing 17th-century Plas Machynlleth, set in parkland to the south.

One of the town's most historic sites is the late medieval **Owain Glyndwr Centre** (Mar–Sept 10am–5pm, Oct–Dec 11am–4pm) in the Parliament House. This building incorporates the remains of an earlier structure in which the Welsh people's hero established the country's first (albeit short-lived) Parliament in 1404. George Borrow lodged at the town-centre Wynstay Hotel during his tour of Wales in 1854 and was waited on by a 'brisk, buxom maid who told me her name was Mary Evans…'.

The **Museum of Modern Art** (MOMA) is in The Tabernacle, a former Wesleyan Chapel (tel: 01654 703355; www.momawales.org.uk; Mon–Sat 10am–4pm; free). The museum has a permanent collection of contemporary

Left: Machynlleth's clock tower is often the central point for events and celebrations, such as New Year's Eve.

Above: the weekly market day in Machynlleth.

artworks, primarily from artists living or working in Wales. There are also temporary exhibitions and concerts.

YNYS-HIR NATURE RESERVE

Although this route ends here, if you have time you might wish to travel just a few miles south-west of Machynlleth where, off the A487 near Eglwysfach, is **Ynys-hir Nature Reserve** (tel: 01654 700222; www.rspb.org.uk; reserve daily 9am–9pm or dusk if earlier; visitor centre Apr–Oct daily 9am–5pm, Nov–Mar daily 10am–4pm). This extensive reserve provides a home for a wide range of birds such as egrets, redshanks and wood warblers. There are seven hides and two circular nature trails, making it a great place for the whole family.

Ⓔ Eating Out

Nr Dolgellau
Penmaenuchaf Hall
Penmaenpool (1½ miles/2.4km west of Dolgellau); tel: 01341 422129; www.penhall.co.uk; daily noon–2.30pm, 7–9pm.
Elegant dining in the garden restaurant of this country hotel combines contemporary features such as Welsh slate floors with white tablecloths and candlelight. A modern British menu features dishes such as local venison with red cabbage, and fillet of pork with black pudding. £££

Aberdyfi
Penhelig Arms
Terrace Road; tel: 01654 767215; www.penheligarms.com; bar and restaurant noon–2pm daily, restaurant 7–9pm daily.
This seafront hotel offers fish dishes in both the restaurant and more relaxed bar area. Dishes might include smoked haddock and salmon fishcakes or pork escalopes with spring onion mash. Vegetarian choices also feature. ££–£££

Machynlleth
Quarry Café
Maengwyn Street; tel: 01654 702624; Mon–Sat 9am–4.30pm.
This café offers plenty of healthy wholefood dishes, made with organic and fair trade produce. There are vegetarian and vegan choices such as veggie burgers and almond risotto. £

Nr Machynlleth
Ynyshir Hall
Eglwysfach (off A487); tel: 01654 781209; www.ynyshirhall.co.uk; lunch daily noon–2pm, dinner daily 7–9pm; booking essential.
This lovely country hotel, with a cosy dining room and glorious views, serves Michelin-starred food, such as oysters with caviar, or scallop and lobster carpaccio to start. Mains might include sea trout with wild garlic gnocchi or braised duck with sherry jus. £££

Travel Tips

Active Pursuits

North Wales, and the Snowdonia National Park in particular, is a marvellous place for getting active. The wild landscape offers rigorous challenges as well as gentle exercise – and whether you're super-fit or a family wanting some fun in the fresh air, there's something to suit you. By far the most popular outdoor pursuit is walking, closely followed by mountain biking and climbing. But you can also enjoy pony trekking, canoeing and kayaking, and even golf.

WALKING

There's an almost bewildering choice of walking routes, ranging from long-distance waymarked paths to forest tracks and nature trails. There are, however, plenty of guidebooks and leaflets available at information centres and bookshops. Climbing Snowdon or Cadair Idris are popular goals but their often-congested paths are

not to everyone's taste – and they're obviously not for novices. Each mountain range enjoys its own distinctive character. In the north the Carneddau offer vast grassy whaleback ridges, while the adjacent Glyders and Tryfan are strewn with frost-shattered boulders. Behind Tremadog Bay rise the Rhinogs, unfrequented mountains of ankle-twisting rock and deep heather. Both the Cadair Idris and Snowdon massifs offer rugged walking, sustained gradients and wonderful views.

By contrast, the featureless and often boggy Migneint between Bala and Ffestiniog is strictly for connoisseurs of solitude. The Aran ridge running north from Dinas Mawddwy to Bala Lake is regaining popularity after access problems. West and north of Blaenau Ffestiniog, the Moelwyns are laced with the fascinating relics of slate mining.

For family groups and the less mobile there are miles of gentler footpaths and bridleways to explore. Good examples may be found in Gwydir Forest around Betws-y-Coed, in Coed-y-Brenin Forest near Dolgellau and around many of Snowdonia's more accessible lakes. The dismantled Welsh Highland Railway at Beddgelert gives an entertaining ramble through several tunnels and there is estuary-edge walking on the Mawddach Trail west of Dolgellau. A coastal path of 125 miles (200km) has been developed around the shoreline of Anglesey, and there is also an 84-mile (146km) path around the edge of the Lleyn Peninsula. Waymarked long-distance trails include the 108-mile (174km) Dyfi Valley Way and the 60-mile (97km) North Wales Path between Prestatyn and Bangor (for information on trails, visit www.walking. visitwales.com).

Of various challenge walks, the most famous is the Welsh 3000s (www. welsh3000s.co.uk), a gruelling 30-mile (48km) tramp over all 15 of Snowdonia's 3,000ft (914m) -plus summits within a 24-hour period.

National Park walks

Details of mountain and leisure walks in Snowdonia National Park appear on the official website: www.eryri-npa.gov.uk, together with details of special events. Some walks also appear in the free visitor magazine *Eryri*. Routes are graded for difficulty and duration. It's important to be properly shod and clothed for walking. Even on low-level paths the weather can change quickly, while on the tops, protection from the elements may become vital for survival. Since the installation of an automatic, solar-powered weather station on Snowdon's summit, with hourly data relayed to base stations by mobile phone, reliable mountain forecasts are now assured (tel: 0870 900 0100; www.metoffice.gov.uk).

Preceding Pages: Anglesey coastal path at Port Trecastell. **Left**: walking from Capel Curig in the Snowdonia National Park. **Below**: the golf course at Nefyn, along the Lleyn Peninsula.

Ⓕ Get Golfing

The North Wales coast is home to some excellent golf courses. The finest is Royal St Davids Golf Club in Harlech (tel: 01766 780361; www. royalstdavids.co.uk), a championship links course that sits beneath Harlech Castle. There are also courses on the Lleyn Peninsula at Abersoch, Nefyn and Pwllheli; a course at Porthmadog and one further down the coast at Aberdyfi – for information see www.golf-northwales.co.uk.

CLIMBING

Snowdonia's great buttresses and gullies have attracted rock climbers in ever greater numbers since before World War I when Colin Kirkus and John Menlove Edwards pioneered audacious new ascents. Later, in the 1950s, the likes of Joe Brown and Don Whillans immortalised such locations as the Llanberis Pass and Snowdon's Clogwyn Du'r Arddu. More recently, interest has spread out from the inland crags to embrace the sea cliffs of Anglesey, the Lleyn Peninsula, Llandudno's Great Orme and the cliffs north of Tremadog. While it is feasible for confident hillwalkers to tackle scrambling routes (requiring the use of hands as well as feet), climbing with ropes should only be attempted by experienced climbers. Courses in hillwalking, climbing, mountaineering and associated sports, including canoeing and kayaking, are provided at Wales's National Mountain Sports Centre at Plas-y-Brenin, Capel Curig (tel: 01690 720214; www.pyb.co.uk).

MOUNTAIN BIKING

Every kind of cycling terrain exists in the Snowdonia region, from meandering back-lanes to severe mountain gradients. Off-road riding is permitted on public bridleways, unclassified roads and on specially waymarked cycle tracks such as those in the Gwydir and Coed-y-Brenin forests. Cycling is not permitted on footpaths or over trackless countryside. Under the National Voluntary Cycling Agreement for Snowdonia, cyclists are requested not to ride up to, or down from, the summit of Snowdon between 10am and 5pm from 1 May to 30 September. There is full access from October to the end of May. A leaflet available at cycle shops, warden centres and tourist information centres outlines alternative routes through mountainous terrain in the Snowdon area. With careful use of an OS map, many worthwhile itineraries 'off the beaten track' can be devised

Below: learn to climb at the National Mountain Sports Centre, Plas-y-Brenin.

Above: canoeing on Lake Bala.

to suit individual abilities. The gentle countryside and quiet country lanes of Anglesey and the Lleyn Peninsula make them ideal for family cycling. Bike hire outlets include: Dolgellau Cycles (The Old Furnace, Smithfield Street, Dolgellau; tel: 01341 423332; www.dolgellau cycles.co.uk); Beics Brenin (Coed-y-Brenin Visitor Centre, Dollgellau; tel: 01341 440728; www.beicsbrenin. co.uk); Beddgelert Bikes (The Bike Barn, Beddgelert Forest; tel: 01766 890434; www.beddgelertbikes.co.uk).

HORSE RIDING

You do not have to be an expert to enjoy pony trekking. Trekking centres will match horses to individual riding ability; the pace is relaxed and younger children can go along too. Riding and hacking are for the more experienced, with trail riding, sometimes over several days, the most adventurous option. Welsh mountain ponies and the smaller Welsh cobs are used at most riding/trekking centres. Access to the countryside is virtually the same as for mountain biking. Regional centres include Snowdonia Riding Stables at Waunfawr, near Caernarfon (tel: 01286 650342; www. snowdoniaridingstables.co.uk) and the Isle of Anglesey Riding Centre at Tal-y-foel farm, near Dwyran on Anglesy (tel: 01248 450377; www.tal-y-foel.co.uk). Visit the Wales Trekking and Riding Association website for further information: www.ridingwales.com.

WATER SPORTS

Snowdonia's long coastline bordering Cardigan Bay and the Irish Sea is a premier venue for dinghy sailing. There are excellent marinas at Conwy, Caernarfon and Pwllheli, as well as numerous sheltered moorings in fishing harbours and bays. Surfing, windsurfing and sea-kayaking are catered for by a coast offering exposure to, or protection from, all points of the compass. For more information contact the National Outdoor Centre (tel: 01248 670964; www.plasmenai. co.uk) at Plas Menai.

Inland, canoeing is enjoyed on mountain lakes and challenging rivers. For suitable locations and prevailing conditions contact the National White Water Centre near Bala (tel: 01678 521083; www.ukrafting.co.uk).

Downhill Adventure

The Llandudno Ski Centre (tel: 01492 874707; www.jnlllandudno. co.uk) is a great place for kids to let off steam – and adults too. There's a dry ski slope, where you can have a go at both skiing and snowboarding (children must be over 4 years of age), as well as a toboggan run which is (2,460ft) 750m long. The centre also has Sno-tubes: inflatable rings which you climb into then ride downhill at high speed.

Themed Holidays

There's plenty of potential for themed breaks in North Wales and the Snowdonia National Park – and there are opportunities for both adults and children. Most options involve exploring the outdoors in some way, but there are more sedate breaks on offer too. The options below will give you some ideas.

ART

The lush landscape of North Wales makes it an ideal spot for painting holidays. Brush Strokes (Dolwyddelan, near Betws-y-coed; tel: 01690 750488; www.brush-strokes.org) runs a wide range of artistic courses, such as watercolour workshops, landscape painting weekends and sketching breaks.

CONSERVATION

Snowdonia is so popular with walkers and cyclists that footpath erosion is a serious problem. So the National Trust often runs working holidays in the area, in which volunteers help to fix footpaths on the mountains. They also run breaks in which volunteers help control invasive species in the countryside – plants like Japanese knotweed and Himalayan balsam. The type of activity varies annually. For information tel: 0844 800 3099; www.nationaltrust.org.uk.

COOKERY

If you want to brush up on your cooking skills while you're on holiday in Wales, then you could sign up for a course at the Bodnant Welsh Food Cookery School in Conwy (tel: 01492 651108; www.bodnant-welshfood.co.uk), where you can learn how to make both Welsh specialities and global cuisines using local ingredients.

Above: children have a wide choice of activities in which to participate.

OUTDOOR ADVENTURE

The Plas-y-Brenin National Mountain Sports Centre in Capel Curig (tel: 01690 720214; www.pyb.co.uk) is at the heart of the Snowdonia National Park and offers a wide range of residential courses in everything from rock climbing and hillwalking to canoeing. Courses cater for a range of abilities: there are courses for those who wish to become mountaineering instructors, as well as ones for families who want an introduction to kayaking.

The National White Water Centre, near Bala (tel: 01678 521083; www.ukrafting.co.uk), offers short courses with accommodation, in which you combine white-water rafting with another activity such as canyoning, rock climbing, mountain biking or clay pigeon shooting. There's also a bushcraft course that teaches you all the essential skills of survival, such as shelter building and water sourcing.

RAILWAY BREAKS

Steam railway fans might want to join one of the driver experience courses run by some of the famous vintage railways in North Wales, offering the opportunity to get 'hands-on' with a real steam locomotive. The Llangollen Railway (tel: 01978 860979; www.llangollen-railway.co.uk), Fairbourne Railway (tel: 01341 250362; www.fairbournerailway.com), and Talyllyn Railway (tel: 01654 710472; www.talyllyn.co.uk) all offer driver experience days.

RETREATS

If you're after some inner peace and love the calm of the countryside, then you might want to join one of the many retreats held at St Bueno's Spirituality Centre, near St Asaph (tel: 01745 583444; www.beunos.com). This former Jesuit college was where poet Gerard Manley Hopkins trained for the priesthood, and where he was inspired to write many of his poems. As well as weekend and week-long retreats, St Beuno's also runs a variety of spirituality courses.

WELSH LANGUAGE

The Welsh language is an ancient Celtic tongue, most closely related to Cornish and Breton *(see p.60)*. It is still widely spoken in North Wales and you can get to grips with its lyrical sounds on an intensive residential course at the Welsh Language Centre, Nant Gwrtheyrn (tel: 01758 750334; www.nantgwrtheyrn.org), on the Lleyn Peninsula. Courses are available for complete beginners, as well as those with some knowledge of the language.

Above: tackling the River Tryweryn at the National White Water Centre.

Practical Information

All the essential practical information you need to make your trip to Snowdonia and North Wales run smoothly.

GETTING THERE

By road

Access from the northwest has been greatly speeded up by completion of the A55 North Wales Expressway which continues beneath the Conwy Estuary to Bangor and Holyhead. For the Vale of Conwy, Betws-y-coed and the Vale of Ffestiniog, take the southbound A470 from Glan Conwy. Thomas Telford's London to Holyhead highway, now the A5, heads west from the M54 via Llangollen to Capel Curig and thence through the mountains to Bethesda and the A55.

Befitting its Roman origins, Caernarfon sits at the hub of radiating roads. The A4085 and A4086 flank Snowdon itself, while the A497/499 strikes southwest for the Lleyn Peninsula.

Two parallel north-south roads link the Vale of Ffestiniog with the River Mawddach, taking in the Cardigan Bay resorts and Coed-y-brenin forest.

Southwest from Bala towards Dolgellau the A494 follows a major geological fault line. Southeastern Snowdonia is approached on the A470 from Llanidloes and Newtown, or the A458 from Shrewsbury.

By coach

National Express operate services and from London and Manchester to Llandudno, Bangor, Caernarfon and Porthmadog, tel: 08717 818181; www.nationalexpress.com. Arriva provide services throughout Wales to Aberystwyth, Carmarthen, Dolgellau, Porthmadog, Caernarfon and Bangor, tel: 0871 200 22 33; www.arrivabus.co.uk.

By train

Train services from London Euston run to Crewe, where passengers can

Above: the B4391, the old pre-power station road from Porthmadog to Bala, strikes out across the Migneint.

change for Holyhead, with stops at Llandudno Junction and Bangor. Other local trains call at Conwy, Penmaenmawr, Llanfairfechan and stations on Anglesey. Blaenau Ffestiniog is reached by a branch line through the Vale of Conwy from Llandudno Junction. From Blaenau Ffestiniog the narrow-gauge Ffestiniog Railway runs down to Porthmadog, connecting at Minffordd station with the scenic Cambrian Coast Line between Pwllheli and Aberystwyth. Services to and from the Midlands via Shrewsbury connect to Machynlleth. For all timetable and fare enquiries, tel: 08457 484950; www.nationalrail.co.uk.

By plane

The nearest international airports to North Wales are Manchester (tel: 08712 710711; www.manchesterairport.co.uk), Liverpool (tel: 0871 521 8484; www.liverpoolairport.com) and Birmingham (tel: 0871 222 0072; www.birminghamairport.co.uk). Cardiff Airport (tel: 01446 711111; www.cardiff-airport.com) has links to airports in Ireland and Scotland, as well as various European destinations. There are flights during the week between Cardiff Airport and Anglesey with Citywing (tel: 0871 200 0440; www.citywing.com).

By ferry

There are ferry services, including a high-speed, car-carrying catamaran, between Ireland and Wales: Dublin and Dun Laoghaire are linked to Holyhead on Anglesey, and there are also services between Rosslare and Fishguard, in South Wales. Stena Line, tel: 08447 707070 www.stenaline.com; Irish Ferries, tel: 08717 300 400; www.irishferries.com.

GETTING AROUND
Public transport

For local bus journeys enquire at a TIC. The Wales Explore Pass gives unlimited access to all mainline train services and most buses, while North Wales Rover tickets allow one day's travel on buses and trains in various

---

ⓖ Going Green

Snowdonia has an excellent network of buses, including the Snowdon Sherpa, a circular service around the northern part of the region giving access to the mountains and main towns (reduced winter timetable). The idea is to reduce the number of cars on the roads in the National Park: www.eryri-npa.gov.uk. Regional services across Anglesey, through the Vale of Conwy, down the Cardigan Bay coast and inland to Machynlleth, provide a relaxed and 'green' way to enjoy the scenery.

Above: the Sherpa buses reduce congestion in the National Park.

Combined with bus routes, narrow-gauge railways and with some careful planning, much of Snowdonia is accessible without a car.

zones across North Wales (tel: 0333 3211 202; www.arrivatrainswales.co.uk). Red Rover bus tickets offer a day's unlimited travel in Gwynedd and Anglesey, some services in Conwy, and Snowdon Sherpa bus travel. For enquiries about public transport in Gwynedd, visit www.gyynedd.gov.uk, or across Wales, tel: 0871 200 2233; www.traveline-cymru.info. For tourist steam trains visit www.greatlittletrainsofwales.co.uk.

By car

Having a car does give you the flexibility to visit the hidden corners of Snowdonia. Car hire is available in Cardiff from various operators, in Llandudno from Avis (tel: 0808 284 5566; www.avis.co.uk), and in Aberystwyth, Carmarthen and Caernarfon from Europcar (tel: 08713 849 900; www.europcar.co.uk).

Cycling

Snowdonia is becoming increasingly easy to explore by bike, with many recreational cycle routes, such as the Mawddach Trail, a 9-mile (14km) route from Dolgellau to Morfa Mawd-

Above: strolling along the Anglesey coastal path at Porth Trecastell.

dach, and trails in Coed-y-brenin. There are mountain-bike trails and easy forestry tracks – SNP visitor centres have information. Bikes can be hired from locations such as Beics Betws in Betws-y-coed, tel: 01690 710766; www.bikewales.co.uk and Cefn Coch Guest House near Tywyn, tel: 01654 712193; www.cefn-coch.co.uk.

FACTS FOR THE VISITOR

Disabled Travellers

Much accommodation in Snowdonia is in older buildings or smaller B&Bs, so lifts are not standard. However, they will be present in larger chain hotels. Always check access on booking and note that some accommodation providers have specially adapted rooms. For information on the best places to stay with disabled access, visit www.goodaccessguide.co.uk. While public railways and buses have access and wheelchair areas, small stations may be unstaffed and lifts may be closed, so check before travelling. Tourism for All provides general information and contacts, tel: 0845 124 9971; www.tourismforall.org.uk. Information for travel within the UK for visitors with disabilities can also be found at www.gov.uk/transport-disabled.

The Snowdonia National Park website (www.eryri-npa.gov.uk) has a section devoted to accessible travel in the region, with details of easy-access car parks and toilets. They also have a programme of countryside wheelchair walks, posted on their website, and guided monthly walks aimed at visually impaired travellers (tel: 01766 772269). Abergele Mobility (www.abergele-mobility.co.uk) have shops in Abergele (tel: 01745 827990) and Llandudno (tel: 01492 877604), and offer wheelchair and mobility scooter hire. There is useful information on various destinations in North Wales at www.disabledholidayinfo.org.uk.

Emergencies

Dial 999 and ask the operator for the appropriate service: Police, Ambulance, Fire Brigade, Coastguard or Mountain Rescue. (NB: mountain rescue call-outs are initiated by the Police.)

Gay and Lesbian Travellers

There are gay communities in North Wales, but the liveliest scene is in the south in Cardiff. The Gay Guide on www.visitcardiff.com has information on gay- and lesbian-friendly bars and events. Aberystwyth holds a lively annual Pride on the Prom event (www.aberpop.co.uk).

Maps

Ordnance Survey Explorer maps 1:25,000 cover Snowdon and Conwy Valley areas (Sheet OL 17), Harlech and Bala areas (Sheet OL 18) and Cadair Idris area (Sheet OL 23). In addition, you may need Explorer 262, 263 (which cover Anglesey), and 253

Above: a good map and compass are essential for walking in Snowdonia.

and 254 (which cover the Lleyn Peninsula).

Opening Hours

Standard business hours are Mon–Fri 9am–5pm or 5.30pm; post offices will

---

Ⓚ Snowdonia for Children

Few places in Britain have such an abundance of visitor attractions as Snowdonia. Most of these are suitable for children and have been described in the main Places section of this guide. They include the region's Great Little Trains (*see Tours 3, 4, 7 and 9*); its slate caverns at Blaenau Ffestiniog (*see Tour 3, p.46*); its underground power station (*see Tour 4, p.54*), and its historical museums. Then there are all the castles, the Centre for Alternative Technology (*see Tour 8, p.94*) and King Arthur's Labyrinth (*see Tour 8, p.93*) – the list goes on.

   For information on self-guided walks suitable for families, call into one of the Snowdonia National Park information centres. Most mountain-

Above: preparing the miniature train at Betws-y-coed.

bike hire centres cater for youngsters and will provide guidance on which trails are suitable. Traditional longbow archery, woodland den building, and stilt walking are some of the activities at the Greenwood Forest Park near Caernarfon, tel: 01248 671493; www.greenwood forestpark.co.uk.

Above: the heraldic dragon is the Welsh national symbol.

also open Sat 9am–noon. Shop core hours are Mon–Sat 9am–5.30pm. In larger towns like Caernarfon, some shops may stay open later, especially in peak season – they may also open on Sunday between 10am and 4pm.

Tourist Information

For more information about visiting Snowdonia, contact either a National Park Centre or a local Tourist Information Centre (TIC).

Snowdonia National Park (SNP) Head Office, Penrhyndeudraeth; tel: 01766 770274; www.eryri-npa.co.uk; National Park Centres: Aberdyfi, tel: 01654 767321; Beddgelert, tel: 01766 890615; Betws-y-coed, tel: 01690 710426; Dolgellau, tel: 01341 422888; Harlech, tel: 01766 780658.

Tourist Information Centres contain a wide range of leaflets and publications, many of them free. In addition to answering public transport enquiries, staff can usually assist with accommodation bookings. Suggestions for eating out, places to visit and details of local events are also offered.

Barmouth: Station Road, tel: 01341 280787; Caernarfon: Oriel Pendeitsh, Castle Street, tel: 01286 672232; Conwy: Rosehill Street, tel: 01492 577566; Dolgellau: Eldon Square, tel: 01341 422888; Holyhead: Terminal 1, Holyhead Port, tel: 01407-762622; Llanberis: 41b High Street, tel: 01286-870765; Llandudno: Mostyn Street, tel: 01492 577577; Porthmadog: High Street, tel: 01766 512981; Pwllheli: Min y Don, Station Square, tel: 01758 613000.

North Wales Tourism, tel: 01492 531731, www.nwt.co.uk; Visit Snowdonia, tel: 01341 281485, www.visit snowdonia.info; The Isle of Anglesey, tel: 01248 713177, www.visitanglesey. co.uk; Llandudno; tel: 01492 577577; www.visitllandudno.org.uk; North East Wales, tel: 01978 292015; www.north eastwales.co.uk.

ⓢ Snowdonia Souvenirs

Traditional crafts can be found in numerous outlets throughout Snowdonia. Carved to make gifts and useful items, slate is a popular souvenir; it is available at craft shops and at such visitor attractions as the Inigo Jones Slateworks near Caernarfon and Blaenau Ffestiniog's slate mines. Portmeirion pottery is well regarded and widely collected; it can be purchased from Portmeirion and other quality gift shops.

Above: local potteries, some part of co-operatives, abound in north Wales.

Accommodation

Snowdonia and North Wales have a wide selection of serviced accommodation, ranging from clean, modest guesthouses to boutique and luxury hotels with every amenity. Many establishments serve dinner as an optional extra, and there may also be special reductions for children. TICs hold details of local accommodation and will help with bookings.

The area also has a great choice of good-value, self-catering cottages, farmhouses, flats, chalets and static caravans. One specialist self-catering agency is Wales Cottage Holidays (Bear Lanes, Newtown, Powys; tel: 01686 628200; www.wales-holidays.co.uk). Snowdonia also has many excellent campsites, costing between £12 and £20 for an overnight pitch.

You could go back to nature and stay in a tipi or a yurt at Eco Retreats (tel: 01654 781375; www.ecoretreats.co.uk), a few miles northeast of Machynlleth. There's no electricity and eco-friendliness is a priority.

The Youth Hostel Association (www.yha.org.uk) has bunkhouses and hostels throughout Snowdonia. To book, call the individual hostel, or telephone 0800 0191 700.

The price codes listed are based on a standard double for one night in peak season, including breakfast. Out of season prices can be much lower and many establishments offer special deals, so check websites before booking.

£££ over £140
££ £80–140
£ under £80

RUTHIN AND THE VALE OF CLYWD

Bach y Graig Farmhouse
Tremeirchion, St Asaph; tel: 01745 730627; www.bachygraig.co.uk.
Wooden beams, oak panelling and an inglenook fireplace impart plenty of character to this farmhouse B&B. There are free-range eggs and freshly baked bread for breakfast. Self-catering accommodation is also available. £–££

Bodlonfa Hall
Rhualt, St Asaph; tel: 01745 585288. Light, comfortable rooms at this country-house B&B. It's set in lovely grounds, with a large pond, and all the rooms have garden views. Breakfast is served in an elegant lounge and features lots of Welsh produce. £

Firgrove
Llanfwrog, Ruthin; tel: 01824 702677; www.firgrovecountryhouse.co.uk.
Beautifully furnished bedrooms at this charming Georgian house, just on the outskirts of Ruthin. The large gardens are well maintained and create a tranquil setting. Excellent evening meals are available if you book in advance. ££

Manorhaus
Well Street, Ruthin; tel: 01824 704830; www.manorhaus.com.
Wonderfully stylish bedrooms and cool modern artworks characterise this excellent restaurant with rooms, situated in a Georgian building. Comfort isn't sacrificed to style, and there are fluffy towels, Egyptian cotton bed linen and sleek bathrooms. ££

Pentre Mawr
Llandyrnog, nr Denbigh; tel: 01824 790732; www.pentremawrcountryhouse.co.uk.
This country house looks traditional, but contains some surprises: you can stay in classic rooms with four-poster beds in the house itself, or opt for luxurious safari-style canvas lodges in the grounds which come with underfloor

heating, rich fabrics and hot tubs. Evening meals are available. £££

LLANDUDNO

Bodysgallen Hall and Spa

2 miles (3km) outside Llandudno; tel: 01492 584466; www.bodysgallen. com.

Luxury all the way at this fine country-house hotel, owned by the National Trust. There's a spa and leisure centre, as well as an elegant restaurant. £££

Escape B&B

48 Church Walks; tel: 01492 877776; www.escapebandb.co.uk.

It may be a Victorian villa, but this boutique B&B has contemporary individually designed rooms, bringing welcome urban chic to Llandudno. Flat-screen TVs and free Wi-fi. ££

The Lighthouse

Marine Drive; tel: 01492 876819; www.lighthouse-llandudno.co.uk.

You get great sea views from this B&B, situated in a 19th-century lighthouse which was built to resemble a fortress. It's perched on Great Orme Head, a couple of miles from Llandudno. ££

St Tudno

North Parade, Promenade; tel: 01492 874411; www.st-tudno.co.uk.

Traditionally decorated, comfortable bedrooms at this luxurious small hotel on the seafront. Alice Liddell – immortalised as Alice in Wonderland – stayed here as a child, and it retains a sense of Victorian grandeur. Lovely sea views from the lounge and excellent food in the restaurant. ££

VALE OF CONWY AND CONWY

Castle Hotel

High Street, Conwy; tel: 01492 582800; www.castlewales.co.uk.

Once a coaching inn, this centrally-located hotel mixes period features, like wood panelling and old beams, with refurbished boutique bedrooms. It serves fine Welsh food in the brasserie-style restaurant. ££

The Quay Hotel and Spa

Deganwy Quay, Deganwy; tel: 01492 564100; www.quayhotel.co.uk.

Contemporary-styled rooms and suites at this waterfront hotel with a spa and swimming pool. Many rooms have great views of Conwy castle –

Above: the striking Victorian exterior of Escape B&B in Llandudno.

you can even go for a penthouse with your own balcony. £££

Sychnant Pass House

Sychnant Pass Road, tel: 01492 596868; www.sychnant-pass-house.co.uk.

There are 12 individually designed bedrooms at this friendly house set in the Sychnant Pass. Public rooms are comfortable and relaxing, pets are welcome and the food is excellent. ££–£££

AROUND BETWS-Y-COED AND SNOWDON

Ffin y Parc Country House

Betws Road, Llanrwst; tel: 01492 642070; www.ffinyparc.co.uk.

Two luxury self-catering cottages set in the grounds of a stone-built country house with a Victorian walled garden. Style is eclectic, with a mix of antique and contemporary furnishings. ££–£££

St Curig's Church

Capel Curig; tel: 01690 720469; www. stcurigschurch.com.

You'll find comfortable en-suite B&B rooms in this converted 19th-century church. Popular with walkers and climbers, there's also a 4-bed bunkroom. The dining room and guest lounge is in the former apse, which boasts a shimmering mosaic ceiling. £

Pen y Gwryd Hotel

Nant Gwynant; tel: 01286 870211; www.pyg.co.uk.

This traditional inn, a one-time base for Everest expedition training, attracts plenty of walkers and climbers who want clean, no frills accommodation with good food. £

Pengwern Country House

Allt Dinas, nr Betws-y-coed; tel: 01690 710480; www.snowdoniaaccommodation.co.uk.

Friendly Welsh-speaking hosts and immaculate rooms set in a Victorian house just a mile (1.6km) from the centre of Betws-y-coed. The rooms

are individually designed – the Richard Gay Somerset bathroom offers the best loo-with-a-view in Wales. ££

Swallow Falls Hotel

Holyhead Road, Betws-y-coed; tel: 01690 710796; www.swallowfallshotel. co.uk.

A convenient base for lovers of the great outdoors. The inn has 15 ensuite bedrooms, and there's also a neighbouring campsite. There's home-cooked food in the tavern bar, and landscaped gardens beside the famous Swallow Falls waterfall. £–££

CEIRIOG VALLEY

The Hand at Llanarmon

Llanarmon Dyffyn Ceiriog; tel: 01691 600666; www.thehandhotel.co.uk.

The beautiful Ceiriog Valley is the setting for this former farm which is now a popular hotel. There are guest rooms in the farmhouse and in converted outbuildings, and excellent food is served in the restaurant. ££

ANGLESEY

Bull's Head Inn

Castle Street, Beaumaris; tel: 01248 810329; www.bullsheadinn.co.uk.

This historic coaching inn, where Charles Dickens once stayed, has cosy refurbished bedrooms, many with original features. If you prefer funkier, more contemporary rooms, you can stay in the stylish Townhouse – a former inn, also on Castle Street. ££

Cleifiog

Townsend, Beaumaris; tel: 01248 811507; www.cleifiogbandb.co.uk.

This 5-star B&B has just three guest rooms, all en suite, one of which has 18th-century wood panelling and lovely views of the Menai Strait. The house was a hospice in the 17th century and later a customs house – they say Thomas Telford stayed here while building the Menai Suspension Bridge. ££

Cleifiog Uchaf

Off Spencer Road, Valley; tel: 01407 741888; www.cleifioguchaf.co.uk.
This restored 16th-century Welsh longhouse has eight en-suite bedrooms. There are cosy public rooms, including a library, and an excellent restaurant serving produce from Anglesey. ££

LLEYN PENINSULA

Gwesty Ty Newydd

Aberdaron; tel: 01758 760207; www.gwesty-tynewydd.co.uk.
There are great sea views from the first-floor bedrooms of this attractive inn, situated beside the beach. Two rooms have been adapted for guests with disabilities, and there's a popular seafood restaurant downstairs. ££

Plas Bodegroes

1 mile (1.6km) west of Pwllheli; tel: 01758 612363; www.bodegroes.co.uk.
With tranquil gardens and individually designed bedrooms, this restaurant with rooms is a peaceful haven on the Lleyn. The Michelin-recommended food is what attracts most guests, but the Georgian manor house is charming in itself. £££

Above: inside the stylish, yet welcoming, Ffynnon townhouse.

PORTMEIRION AND FFESTINIOG

Portmeirion Hotel and Castell Deudraeth

Portmeirion; tel: 01766 770000; www.portmeirion-village.com.
There are two hotels at Portmeirion, both offering luxurious accommodation in the magical setting of this Italianate village. £££

Tyddyn du Farm

Gellilydan, Ffestiniog, nr Porthmadog; tel: 01766 590281; www.snowdonia-farm-holidays-wales.co.uk.
This working sheep farm has high-quality accommodation in spacious barn suites with countryside views. Full breakfast is served in the farmhouse, or opt for a lighter version in your suite. ££

ABERDYFI

House Bodfor

Bodfor Terrace, Aberdyfi; tel: 01654 767475; www.lletybodfor.co.uk.
Tastefully designed rooms at this boutique B&B, situated in a town house on the seafront. There are roll-top baths, sea views and organic breakfasts. ££

SOUTHERN SNOWDONIA

Ffynnon

Love Lane, Dolgellau; tel: 01341 421774; www.ffynnontownhouse.com
This town house has five differently styled bedrooms which mix contemporary style with some antique pieces. Great bathrooms with power showers. ££

Tyddynmawr Farmhouse

Cader Road, Dolgellau; tel: 01341 422331, www.wales-guesthouse.co.uk.
There are two bedrooms at this five star B&B outside Dolgellau. One room has great views of Cadair Idris, the other has access onto the patio. A Welsh breakfast is served in the farmhouse. £

Index

Credits

Insight Great Breaks Snowdonia &
North Wales
Written by: Rebecca Ford
Updated by: Rachel Lawrence
Edited by: Sarah Clark
Picture Editor: Tom Smyth
Maps: Phoenix Mapping and Apa
Cartography Department
Production: Rebeka Davies
Series Editor: Rachel Lawrence

All pictures by William Shaw/Apa Publications
except: Alamy 10R, 58B, 59, 86, 102B,
103T, 116; Mike Bean 104; Bigstock 112;
Cadwalladers 11T; Corbis 58T, 85B; Courtesy
Caws Mynddu Cheese 10L; Denis Egan 119;
Hafod Eryri 57C/B; Mary Evans 38B, 103B;
Fotolia 24, 29T, 32, 33, 34, 35, 55T, 81B, 85T,
96B, 100, 113; Alan Harris 26; iStock 2/3,
6/7, 12/13, 22/23, 28T, 38T, 48/49, 75T/B,
77B/T, 81T, 115, 121T; Ian Parkes 41B;
Arwell Parry 15T; Gary Pollmillr 15B; Courtesy
Purple Moose 11B, 45B; Rex Featues 38-39;
Mark Rowland 114; Stemonitis 25CR; Topfoto
38C; James West 93L; Public domain 73, 95B

Cover pictures by: (front) 4Corners Images
(T), William Shaw/Apa (BL & BR); (back)
iStock (T) William Shaw/Apa (C&B)

CONTACTING THE EDITORS: As every
effort is made to provide accurate information
in this publication, we would appreciate it
if readers would call our attention to any
errors and omissions by contacting:
Apa Publications, PO Box 7910,
London SE1 1WE, England.
insight@apaguide.co.uk

Information has been obtained from sources
believed to be reliable, but its accuracy
and completeness, and the opinions based
thereon, are not guaranteed.

© 2015 Apa Publications (UK) Ltd
First Edition 2010
Second Edition 2015
Printed in China by CTPS

Contains Land-Form Panorama Contours
& Meridian 2 and OS Street View data
© Crown copyright and database right.

Worldwide distribution enquiries:
APA Publications GmbH & Co. Verlag KG
(Singapore Branch)
7030 Ang Mo Kio Ave 5,
08-65 Northstar @ AMK, Singapore 569880
apasin@singnet.com.sg
Distributed in the UK by:
Dorling Kindersley Ltd
A Penguin Group company
80 Strand, London, WC2R 0RL, UK
sales@uk.dk.com
Distributed in the United States by:
Ingram Publisher Services
1 Ingram Boulevard, PO Box 3006
La Vergne, TN 37086-1986
ips@ingramcontent.com

INSIGHT GUIDES

INSPIRING YOUR NEXT ADVENTURE

Insight Guides offers you a range to match your needs. Whether inspiration for planning a trip, cultural information, walks and tours, great listings, or practical advice, we have a product to suit you.

www.insightguides.com